MOVE THE BALL

HOW THE GAME OF AMERICAN FOOTBALL CAN HELP YOU ACHIEVE YOUR LIFE GOALS

Jennifer A. Garrett

Move the Ball:
How the Game of American Football Can Help You Achieve Your Life Goals

End Zone Publishing

ISBN: 0988786923
ISBN-13: 9780988786929
Library of Congress Control Number: 2012956204
CreateSpace, North Charleston, South Carolina

First Edition

Printed in the USA

Table of Contents

MOVE THE BALL

HOW THE GAME OF AMERICAN FOOTBALL CAN HELP YOU ACHIEVE YOUR LIFE GOALS

Jennifer A. Garrett

Foreword

Jennifer Garrett is a leader, pure and simple. When I met Jennifer, it was clear right away that Jennifer was different: she possessed that rare quality of communicating through her actions as well as her words. While many of her personal skills were obvious—excellent listening skills, persistent drive, infectious humor and enthusiasm, clarity of thought and expectations, incisive intelligence—how those skills were woven together to create a great leader was not.

But Jennifer was more than just a good leader (I know, because while I watched her out-perform her peers at work, I also heard hilarious running narratives about her children, learned that she liked to play as hard as she worked, and marveled at her as she completed a law degree—and passed the bar exam—in that same time period). In short, Jennifer had a joy for life, and she seemed, more than most people, to invest her best efforts in her most important priorities. What I was not aware of was this: Jennifer had a secret.

What I didn't know was that Jennifer was a serious sports fan, but *not* your everyday, run-of-the-mill sports fan. When Jennifer went to a football game, she didn't just watch the game; she used the game as a window into her life. She was as much a translator as a spectator of the game—she was able to see in the struggles and victories on the field the life lessons needed for victory in her life. So when Jennifer screamed at the umpire or referee, got hoarse for yelling the fight songs, painted her face, did her dance, ate the barbeque, or cried in disappointment, it was not just about the game. Rather, it was the clear reinforcement of those life lessons—displayed to her in bold relief on the field—that enabled her to enjoy the game to the fullest, and yet become strengthened and empowered at the same time.

So Jennifer's joy for life was a natural consequence of the links she observed between talent and performance, and her ability to perform at a consistently high level flowed directly from the connections she was able to draw between effort and character. Her leadership skill was constantly being renewed and refined as she applied the lessons she learned to teamwork and winning.

So this book is Jennifer's great gift. It presents an amazing, yet very simple approach to winning in life. By applying the insights she has gained to her own life, she set herself apart, successfully leading difficult, high-pressure teams to victory under stressful circumstances. But she did so without losing herself—winning in life as well as in the game. That's why this book is so important. It's important to listen to Jennifer, because Jennifer has a message to anyone seeking to lead a life of achievement as well as balance. The insights contained in this book present leadership as an ever-present art that can be observed and appreciated, and they prove that the mantle of leadership can be worn by anyone.

By the way, if Jennifer is correct in arguing that the more one comes to love sports, the more meaning one can bring to one's life, then that's worth this book alone.

—James E. Braggs,
Quality Black Belt Expert

Preface

The game of American football is like none other. Many people consider it not only the best sport in America, but also the best sport in the world. From players' Cinderella stories to teams' spectacular comeback victories, football affects people's lives in a constructive way.

This sport teaches us about life; like football, life is a game of strategy and teamwork. The principles football teaches both on and off the field are the same ones we need to achieve our personal and career goals. I learned this at an early age and these doctrines have been a driving force in why I have been able to accomplish my goals while facing a myriad of challenges.

My story is not unique. Everyone has obstacles to achieving greatness. Everyone handles those barriers in different ways. Some people find ways to overcome them. Others make excuses and never realize their dreams.

People often tell me that they're amazed at my accomplishments. They share how they wish they had done one thing or another in their lives. I respond by telling them that they can. It's never too late to get into the end zone and score. I have shared with these individuals the principles highlighted within this book and how they will help them get what they want in life. At the end of our conversations, they have been inspired to move forward toward their goals. I want this book to do the same for you.

Dedication

Thank you to my family and friends who have been *with me* along my journey of writing this book. You have energized me to move the ball forward.

This book intentionally has twenty-six chapters because it was my son Anfernee's football jersey number when I finished this book. Anfernee, his Forest Hills Northern High School teammates, and the coaching staff played an instrumental role in some of the principles described throughout this book. There are also hundreds of other football athletes that I have never met and yet have been moved by their stories. To these elite players, you have and will continue to achieve greatness. Thank you for inspiring me.

Chapter 1:

Introduction

Football taught me about life. Every goal I have achieved was tied to the principles of this game. As a quarterback in the game of life, I know what getting blindsided felt like. I have been knocked down by the blitz. Because I know football inside and out, I use the strategies from the game to accomplish my goals. Football trained me how to beat life's challenges. It will show you how to do the same. You only live once, so play the game like a great athlete. Move the ball and make your dreams a reality.

Walk into any bookstore or search online retailers, and you'll find numerous books comparing running a business to a team sport. Most of these books concentrate on how to be a good leader, how to gain market share, and how to differentiate your business. This book differs from other sports-related books because it's not about your business, or your career...it's about *you*–the whole person. It looks at you, the individual, in ways that speak to the core of you are. It will challenge you to find your identity and your vision.

As the quarterback on your life's field, you must make decisions that will get you into the end zone. Defenders will test your ability to cross the goal line. Football can show you how to get past them and how to win in life, just like it showed me. This book will walk you through these principles and show you how to apply them on your personal field.

As a kid, I loved football—it was my passion. All I ever wanted to do was play football. During my senior year at a new high school, I drummed up enough courage to talk to the coach about joining the football team. At five-foot three, and 120 lbs, I was not a big kid. And...I was a girl. Neither my dad nor the coach thought it was a good idea.

Though I didn't make the team, it didn't change my love for the game. While other girls worried about their hair and what to wear to homecoming, I surrounded myself with football. Instead of hanging out with the popular girls, I ate lunch with the football players. We talked about previous games and reviewed the playbook, examining what worked and what didn't. That was my life. As I got older, my hunger for the game only increased. I needed football, and my life was incomplete without it.

Football consumed my existence.

Football taught me how to succeed. When navigating through life's challenges, I knew what the playbook needed to be to get into the end zone and score. Despite the challenges of teenage pregnancy and single parenthood, I learned how to scramble in the pocket, get past defenders, and move the ball forward on my life's football field.

To move the ball forward, I knew I needed an education. I earned bachelor's degrees in Electrical Engineering and in Biomedical and Clinical Engineering. While working fulltime and raising four children, I pursued graduate degrees. I have master's degrees in Business Administration and in Communication and Leadership Studies. The lessons I learned from football helped me do it. I also decided to go for a law degree, and won that game by the time I was thirty-one. That's the benefit of having a game plan for life.

I now serve as a judge advocate in the Army National Guard JAG Corps and am a marketing director for General Electric. And I still love football.

Great football athletes and coaches know football focuses beyond winning in a single game or a single season. Throughout the seasons of my life, I've continued to use football to excel.

Are you where you want to be in life? Is your game plan sound? What's in your playbook?

Move the Ball will help you define and accomplish your life's goals. It will use powerful examples to uncover the similarities between life and football. By providing insights and analogies to the personal side of life, as well as offering a perspective on choices we make in our careers, this book will show you how you can realize all of your desires. It will show you how to win.

How badly do you want to achieve your goals? Come with me on this journey down your football field of life. Together we will get into the end zone, and you *will* score.

It's almost game time—get fired up!

Chapter 2:
The Pre-Game Show

"The difference between ordinary and extraordinary is that little 'extra.'"
—Jimmy Johnson

We risked our lives driving to Chicago the night before the big day. Visibility outside was as clear as a murky swamp. Cars skidded along the snow-covered, icy roads, and trucks swerved to avoid crashing. I firmly gripped the passenger's side *oh-shit* handle for most of the ride. We were among the lucky ones. After a distressing four-hour car drive, we had made it to our destination untouched.

On January 23, 2011, thousands of football fans poured through the gates of Soldier Field to watch the greatest football game of the postseason—The National Football Conference (NFC) championship game between the Chicago Bears and the Green Bay Packers.

A tsunami of energy hit the inside of the shuttle as it transported us from the parking garage to the stadium. People eagerly held onto their crazy signs, waiting for their chance to display them to the crowd as well as get their five seconds of national television fame. A guy sitting across from me tried to pump up the crowd: "Ditka...Mustache...Polish sausage..."

This game was between the NFL's oldest rivalry: *Da Bears* and *The Cheeseheads.* The experience of cheering alongside thousands of your closest friends was indescribable.

As I walked into Soldier Field stadium, my smile was as big as the Cheshire Cat's. I was bundled in layers of clothing, like everyone around me. At that moment, no one cared that it was seventeen degrees outside.

Football fans understood how important this game was. On that Sunday afternoon nothing else mattered. And on that Sunday, either team could win.

The Bears and the Packers had not played each other in such a postseason game since the Western Division playoffs at Wrigley Field on Sunday, December 14, 1941. Nearly seventy years later, these two teams were fighting for the ultimate prize: the winner received admission to play in Super Bowl XLV and a shot at winning the Lombardi Trophy.

The Chicago Bears dominated the NFL in the 1940s. They proved to football fans everywhere why *Da Bears* earned the song "Bear Down, Chicago Bears!" The 1985 Bears were unstoppable, and they destroyed the New England Patriots to win Super Bowl XX. Final Score: 46–10.

My eyes were cemented to the television during that entire game. Though I was only seven, I understood the importance of the Super Bowl.

Can my Chicago Bears make it to the Super Bowl yet again? I'd wondered over the seasons that followed. And sometimes, the Bears gave me reason to wonder. Year after year, the city of Chicago hoped for another championship team. The dream had never materialized.

"Maybe next year," we'd always say.

Then, in 2011—twenty-five years after the Bears' last Super Bowl victory, Chicago was ready for the Monsters of the Midway to give us something to remember. We had the Bears fight song. We had the Super Bowl Shuffle. We needed something else.

The crowd started to get louder. It was game time.

First play…Packers quarterback Aaron Rodgers threw a pass deep right to Greg Jennings for twenty-two yards. The Packers were moving the ball.

Second play…Aaron Rodgers threw a pass deep middle to Jennings for a twenty-six-yard gain.

Oh shit. Packers were now on the Bears thirty-six-yard line. Soon they would be in the red zone.

Five plays later, they scored a touchdown. Packers 7, Bears 0.

This was not starting off well. The Packers had capitalized on the fundamentals of football and gotten into the end zone first.

The teams continued to battle it out on the football field. With less than ten minutes to go in the game, the Packers were leading by two touchdowns. Reality sank in, and the Bears' likelihood of a Super Bowl appearance was dismal.

A renewed wave of energy invigorated the crowd as the Bears scored their second touchdown. They were only seven points behind—it wasn't over yet. The game went on.

The Bears struggled and were facing fourth and five with less than two minutes remaining in the game. The Bears *had* to go for it here. They called a time-out.

I looked around the stadium. Everyone knew what was riding on this game. Many fans had put their lives in jeopardy to get to Chicago. We stood there like frozen popsicles as we eagerly waited for the game to resume. A moment like this one was why we put our lives at risk.

Similar to life, football is about making choices. It's about choosing and then successfully executing the play in the playbook that

> Winning the games of life and football requires executing the playbook and moving the ball forward.

has the highest chance of moving the ball forward—of getting that next first down.

Here, the million-dollar question was, *If I was Head Coach Lovie Smith and Offensive Coordinator Mike Martz, what play would I run?* Every fan had an idea. I had an idea. If the Bears didn't get this first down, the game would effectively be over.

As the late Los Angeles Lakers' commentator Chick Hearn would often say at Lakers games, "This game's in the refrigerator! The door's closed, the lights are out, the eggs are cooling, the butter's getting hard, and the Jell-O is jiggling..."

There could be no door closing here. The Bears could not let the Packers win.

If you were the coach, what would you do? Would you have them run down the middle or perhaps throw a short pass? Would you try something else? It's your call, but so much is riding on it. You can barely hear yourself think over the noise in the stadium.

So much was at stake.

The Bears didn't win that game. As I slumped in the passenger seat of our SUV, exhausted and with a sore throat from the yelling and cussing, I reflected on what football had taught me as a kid. I considered how it had helped me grow and mature into the person I had become.

The Bears' fourth-down scenario is similar to what a person faces in the game of life. Every day we make decisions. The plays we choose from our playbook are critical. As that high school kid on the side line, I used the doctrines of the game of football to tackle any obstacle, beat any blitz, and overcome any blindside on my life's football field. I developed my playbook and moved the ball. I got into the end zone and scored.

I listened to the radio as we drove from Chicago back to Grand Rapids. Bears fans voiced their frustrations. I quickly tired of hearing the criticisms of quarterback Jay Cutler, and the questions surrounding his toughness. Though he'd proved ineffective during the game, his detractors' comments had no merit. The Bears had lost, but Jay Cutler had been only part of the problem.

I turned the volume on the radio down. I closed my eyes and compared my life to the Bears game. Both needed teamwork in order to be successful. In that day's game, there'd been poor play calling and questionable decision-making. That was why they'd lost.

While it's easy to criticize the Bears, this game is no different from other situations in my own life. There were many situations in my past when alternative decisions would have yielded a more favorable outcome, such as making smarter friend choices in high school to choosing better relationship partners in life. On my life's football field, my current field position sometimes started on my own two-yard line. How was I going to move that ball ninety-eight more yards to get into the end zone? What plays should I run to move the ball downfield?

If you were the quarterback and it was your football field, what decisions would you make? Would you read blitz? If so, how would you adjust? On your life's field, you control your ball movement. You must know who is on the field with you and be prepared to answer questions like these if you want to progress forward.

> You are the quarterback. The game is your life.
>
> What decisions are you going to make to move the ball and get into the end zone?

Football showed me how to answer these questions. I use this game to drive everything I do. Even on that cold January evening, these thoughts ran through my head as I watched the

NFC Championship game. The previous month I had changed jobs, switched companies, and moved from Southern California to Western Michigan. We had no family or friends in Grand Rapids and it was an unfamiliar city. While we faced a number of unknowns, I was determined to not let them deter me from progressing forward. My goal was to succeed in my new position and get my family acclimated to the Midwestern culture. Similar to football, I needed to develop my playbook and make decisions that would move our ball downfield and cross the goal line.

This book will help you do the same. *Move the Ball* centers on you and what you want in life. Not on what Wall Street or corporate managers expect of you. Follow your life's dreams and let football help you achieve your goals.

Gale Sayers was a phenomenal college and professional football athlete. At the University of Kansas, he was two time All-American. In 1963, he set an NCAA Division IA record with a 99-yard run against the Nebraska Cornhuskers. As a first-round draft pick for the Chicago Bears, he was named National Football League (NFL) Rookie of the Year.

> "*I learned that if you want to make it bad enough, no matter how bad it is, you can make it.*"
> —Gale Sayers

He holds many NFL records, including becoming the youngest individual inducted in the NFL Hall of Fame (in 1977). Sayers is also a successful businessman after football. He believed in himself. And that made all the difference.

There really is something to be said about believing in yourself. If you do not commit within, your chances of succeeding are limited. In my life, I could have given up many times. But I didn't because I *wanted* it. I didn't care how much hard work or sacrifice was required. I wasn't going to let *anyone or anything* stop me from winning. Football showed the importance of believing in yourself.

I'm the football enthusiast of the household. I holler at the television on Saturdays, Sundays, Mondays, and sometimes on Thursdays during football season.

"What the F***? You moron, how could you drop the football?" I scream.

"Rule No. 1: Protect the Ball, Dumbass."

Though I may be yelling on those game days, the principles of football drive me every day.

"There goes Jen, talking about football again," they sigh. If they don't say it aloud, they're surely thinking it.

"Did you know Calvin Johnson is one of six wide receivers to get more than forty-five touchdowns and fifty-five-hundred yards in his first five NFL seasons?"

"No. But we really don't care. It's the Lions, so who cares anyway?" they'd say dismissively.

My friends didn't quite understand why talking about football was so important to me. Through my childhood and adult years, I have connected football's lessons to life and used them to succeed. This is what separated me from the teenage boys on the football field in high school. It's what separates me from others today. Football means *more* to me than simply the game of football. The parallels between the game and our lives are noteworthy.

The Detroit Lions are an up-and-coming team. As a Chicago Bears fan, I want the Lions to lose. But credit should go where credit is due. Calvin Johnson is explosive. He is one of the hottest wide receivers in the league. Matt Stafford continues to improve, with his great arm-strength and accuracy. These guys know how to move the ball forward.

While certain football teams, like the Lions, didn't stir conversations with my friends, others piqued their interest.

"Hey guys, do you remember back in 2010 when the Bears played the Cowboys? Tony Romo threw two bizarre interceptions, the running game was absent, and their defense failed to protect their two early leads?"

"Yeah but…"

All of sudden it's time to talk football? People don't get it.

The same parallels to life are drawn when talking about the Dallas Cowboys. Execution, teamwork, persistence—these were elements the Cowboys had needed to win in that 2010 game, but had lacked. In the next Bears-Cowboys matchup in 2012, the Cowboys again lacked these winning principles. Tony Romo threw five interceptions. The team couldn't execute the playbook. That's why they lost.

> *"All I know is we have a long way to go,"*
> —Dallas Cowboys owner Jerry Jones after losing to the Chicago Bears, Oct. 1, 2012

The same holds true for the Chicago Bears during the 2012 season. For a team that started off with a 7–1 record, fans were disappointed the Bears couldn't finish strong enough to get into the playoffs. Poor decision-making and lack of playbook execution played a significant part in this outcome. There were other reasons, too, and adjustments must be made by the Cowboys and the Bears if they want a different result for the 2013 postseason.

Achieving your personal goals is no different than playing a football game. Throughout your life, you will face obstacles. Challenges may sometimes seem overpowering. Football will show you how to overcome them and drive the ball forward. It will teach you how to win.

We get one shot on this Earth. Make it count and live with no regrets. Whether you are unhappy in your job or wanting to go back to school, don't look back and say, *What if?* Don't settle; look forward—define your goals, develop your playbook, execute your playbook, and win.

If you ask a coach, a player, or a fan to define football, the answer is different. But at the core, football encompasses *hard work, teamwork, discipline, and dedication to a cause.* Life was hardly meant to be relaxed and uneventful. Neither was football. If either of them were, they would be quite boring.

Mike Ditka was a dynamic head coach. I witnessed his hot-tempered demeanor though his eleven seasons with the Bears, as well as his three with the New Orleans Saints. What made Ditka so intriguing was not only his animated coaching style, but also his accomplishments as a player and a coach.

> *"If things came easy, then everybody would be great at what they did, let's face it."*
> —Mike Ditka

After Ditka left the University of Pittsburgh and signed on with the Chicago Bears, his fifty-eight receptions made an immediate impact on the team. Ditka earned the NFL Rookie of the Year award. He continued to execute the playbook and help the team score. Ditka earned trips to the Pro Bowl each of his remaining seasons with the Bears.

Ditka also made history as one of only two people to win Super Bowls as a player, an assistant coach, and a head coach: he played in the 1963 title championship as well as head coached in the 1985 Bears Super Bowl victory. Though Ditka experienced success both as a player and coach, there were challenges. Winning required hard work, teamwork, discipline, and dedication.

One of my friends told me without the bad, the good wouldn't be great. It's true. We need challenges to value our accomplishments, to experience the joy and elation of winning against obstacles. A great person's true character is displayed when he is able to face adversity, persevere, and accomplish his goals. Football taught me how to do this.

The John Tyler High School Lions can also relate.

On Saturday, November 26, 1994, two days after Thanksgiving, tens of thousands of fans packed into Texas Stadium in Irving, Texas, to watch the undefeated John Tyler Lions play the undefeated Plano East Panthers.

During the first half, nothing spectacular occurred. The team traded scores until the Lions received a 21–14 lead before halftime.

In the second half, the Lions continued to score. With barely three minutes left to play, the Lions were safely ahead, 41–17.

No one in the stadium could prepare for what happened next.

Plano East scored their first touchdown of the half when Terrance Green booted the first of what would become three successful onside kicks. Mickey Jones received Green's first onside kick and headed downfield, only to be stripped of the ball. Panthers recovered. Plano East drove downfield, resulting in a five-yard touchdown pass and subsequent two-point conversion.

Green kicked two more onside kicks, both fumbled by John Tyler's Roderick Dunn. The Panthers scored off both turnovers. Score: John Tyler: 41, Plano East, 44.

Holy shit. What the heck just happened?

It seemed the Panthers were going to pull off an amazing comeback victory. Plano East managed to score four touchdowns in the closing minutes, three of which came from successfully recovering onside kicks.

Announcers claimed this game was "the greatest comeback of all time…of all time."

With only twenty-four seconds left in the game, the John Tyler Lions saw their storybook season nearing the final chapter. Spectators watched in awe.

In a matter of moments, the Lions' surefire win had washed away. The Lions now faced reality. If the game closed with this score, they would hang up their jerseys for the school year.

"I'll be honest, on the way out [to the final kickoff] I was thinking about starting soccer practice," commented Marc Broyles, 1994 John Tyler defensive tackle, to the *Tyler Paper*.

The game clock had not yet expired. Plano East kicked deep. Roderick Dunn, the Lion's senior who had lost control of the second and third onside kicks, caught the final Panthers' kickoff at the three-yard line and sprinted down the east sideline, nearly untouched, to score the final touchdown. Final score: Lions 48, Panthers 44.

The Lions went on to defeat Lake Highlands HS 27–7, Arlington HS 45–20, and finally Austin Westlake HS 35–24 to win the Division II state title. Of the 555 games played in Texas Stadium before it closed, this game is known as one of the most memorable in its history.

The Lions players appreciated the victory more because they had to work for it. Football taught the boys and everyone watching that day an important lesson: *Do not quit playing until the game clock reads 00:00. Never stop believing that you can win.*

This book is organized into three themes: Planning, Acting, and Believing. In life and in football, achieving your goals requires the following:

1) developing your goals and your playbook (planning),
2) executing that playbook (acting), and
3) having the courage and confidence to progress forward
   (believing).

Throughout this book, I will be highlighting my own experiences, as well as various football examples to illustrate how strategies of football will help you win.

Imagine you are the quarterback on your life's football field. The ball is placed on your own twenty-yard line. There are eighty yards to go, and a team of defenders stands between you and the goal line. How would *you* play the game in order to score that touchdown? How would *you* secure good field position to attempt a field goal? If it were fourth down, what would be *your* next move?

> *"To accomplish great things, we must not only act but also dream, not only plan but also believe."*
> —Anatole France, 1921 Winner of the Nobel Prize in Literature

Football is exciting because the great players in this sport don't just settle for being ordinary. They have a strong belief in themselves and strive to be extraordinary. They have MAD PRIDE. I want you to train like an athlete and develop MAD PRIDE, too. These eight elements will help you reach greatness. Each of them will be covered in detail later in this book. By applying these principles to your goals, you will succeed and achieve greatness. The time is *now* to move the ball and make a change. So, approach life with that extra something, and become extraordinary.

Coach's Chalkboard – Get Fired Up!

* Winning football games and winning the game of life is about:

  - defining the goals & developing the playbook
  - executing the playbook
  - having MAD PRIDE to move the ball forward

* Winning the game isn't easy, it requires hard work, teamwork, discipline and dedication

* You are the quarterback. How are you going to move the ball?

Chapter 3:

Are You *With Me?*

"Football is an honest game. It's true to life. It's a game about sharing. Football is a team game. So is life." —Joe Namath

Baseball is America's favorite pastime, but football is America's passion.

When the players step onto the football field, energy consumes the stadium. No matter whom the game is between, vast amounts of hype and trash-talking have occurred in the weeks leading up to the event.

The moment of truth has come. While no one can predict the winner, everyone hopes that his or her team will come out on top. Regardless of the outcome, one fundamental principle always holds true: *Dedicated teamwork amongst the players is necessary to achieve the win.*

A talented quarterback cannot win by himself alone—and neither can you.

The Canadian Football League (CFL) differs from American football in a few ways. One important distinction is that Canadian teams only have three attempts to get a first down. This design drives the need for a passing offense. While the NFL has more liberty to run short passes, its paradigm has shifted. The NFL is now a strong passing league. College football is no different. The spread offense now dominates at schools once known for having a running-game mentality.

> **2011 NFL Season**
>
> ✓ NFL teams averaged an all-time high of 229.7 yards per game
>
> ✓ NFL average passer ratings, number of attempts, and yards-per-attempt at all-time highs
>
> ✓ NFL teams fielded ten 4,000-yard passers (double from 2010)
>
> ✓ Drew Brees, Tom Brady, and Matt Stafford surpassed 5,000-yard mark
>
> ✓ The NFL had more 1,000-yard receivers (19) than 1,000-yard rushers (15)

When you're in a passing league, you need at least one top-notch receiver to make those remarkable plays. Life requires a strong passing game as well. You cannot move the ball without other players. Dangerous quarterback–wide receiver tandems are necessary to win.

While this principle is understood across the NFL, in 2012, three teams were proactive and used their franchise tag on wide receivers before free agency opened. The Eagles kept DeSean Jackson, the Patriots retained Wes Welker, and the Chiefs held onto Dwayne Bowe. These franchises took extra measures to secure their strong quarterback-receiver combos. These pairs are an essential element to the teams' playbooks.

During the mid-1980s, the most potent offensive duo was arguably the San Francisco 49ers' Joe Montana and Jerry Rice. During their eight seasons playing together, Montana and Rice won two Super Bowl championships, and made seven trips to the postseason. Rice was the benchmark for wide receivers to come.

While the Montana-Rice days are ones many football fans will never forget, plenty of other quarterback–wide receiver tandems have also excited football fans.

Two great pairs of the past were Dallas Cowboys' Troy Aikman and Michael Irvin, and the Indianapolis Colts' Peyton Manning and Marvin Harrison.

> **Jerry Rice NFL Stats**
>
> ✓ 1985 NFL Rookie of the Year
>
> ✓ During second NFL season, led NFL with 1,570 receiving yards and 15 TDs
>
> ✓ 1,549 career receptions for 22,895 yards and 208 career TDs
>
> ✓ Currently holds NFL records in career receptions, receiving yards, and receiving touchdowns

And there were more. Jay Cutler and Brandon Marshall were together for three years in Denver (2006–2008). They both made their first Pro Bowl trips in their last season together. They have once again reunited in Chicago for the 2012 season, and the Bears offense has been solid.

In 2010, the Eagles' Michael Vick and DeSean Jackson were unquestionably one of the NFL's most explosive tandems, averaging 23.5 yards per pass, a league best. Typically pass rushers can get to the quarterback in four seconds. With Vick's instincts and ease of mobility, he extends the play past this window, allowing Jackson more time to get free down the field. These two continue to make dangerous plays. They use each other's strengths to execute the Eagle's playbook. In your life, you'll also need strong receivers to help you get into the end zone.

The Patriots' Tom Brady and Wes Welker are equally as dangerous. Brady is comfortable in the pocket, because he can read the coverage and knows what to do before the ball is snapped. Welker is incredibly physical and explosive, and he led the 2011 NFL season in receptions. This duo is unstoppable; they're aligned, and they can use the team's coverage to connect.

Each of these pairs is unique. They bring different skills and strengths to the game, but they share one common theme: They're committed to winning and play as a team to win.

Winning your life's goals requires the same mentality.

However, a strong quarterback and a game-changing receiver alone do not win football games. Nine other players on the offense must also be focused on moving the ball forward.

I often preach to my friends and colleagues that on any given day, any team can win. It's very true. The Green Bay Packers played the Indianapolis Colts in the fifth week of the 2012 football season. The Colts were the underdog. By halftime, the Packers were winning 21-3. When the game ended, the Colts had won 30-27. The Colts' head coach Chuck Pagano wasn't on the field that day. He watched the game from his hospital room as he battled leukemia. The players *wanted* this win, and they never gave up. The team won this game for Chuck.

Football taught me the importance of teamwork. As a kid I watched the Bears come back from twenty-point deficits. I learned valuable lessons from those games.

Lesson 1: *You must play the entire game.*
Lesson 2: *You must be committed.*
Lesson 3: *You need a team to win.*

In my career and personal life, I accomplished my goals because of others. Life is a team sport. It's not a one-man game.

My sixteen-year-old son, Anfernee, plays football at Forest Hills Northern (FHN) High School in Grand Rapids, Michigan. I went to my first football open house at the end of his sophomore year. I didn't know what to expect. When I left that evening, I was fired up and ready for the next football season to start.

I mingled with other parents until 6:30 p.m., when head coach Jeff Rapelje requested all parents to take a seat in the auditorium for some announcements. Coach Rap started the meeting by praising the Husky football team and his talented coaching staff.

Coach Rap explained his goal for the upcoming football season. He wanted the Huskies to make it to the Michigan State High School Football Championships. This was a lofty goal for a team that had finished the prior season with a 5–4 record—and this had been their best record since 2002. In fact, in 2007, the Huskies had gone winless.

While a state championship didn't appear promising, I was pleased with the stretch goal.

Coach was setting the bar high, and he was focused on pushing this football team. He was striving for greatness.

Making the championships did not matter to me. What invigorated me was the coach's commitment to challenging these boys. He wanted to stretch them beyond their comfort zones. While I was excited, I was not prepared for what he said next.

Four words came out of his mouth: *Are you with me?*

Hard work would be required to achieve Coach Rap's goal. So would sacrifice.

Similar to other football teams, the Huskies conditioned through the off-season. During the summer, the boys trained in sweltering heat over the summer, including intense two-a-day practices in August. With Michigan's humidity, the risk of injury was severe.

According to a study coauthored by University of Georgia climatologist Andrew Grundstein, deaths of high school football players in the US nearly tripled between 1994 and 2009, as compared to the preceding fifteen-year period. On average, nearly three football players died each year in practice sessions due to overheating, or hyperthermia.

Coach Rap concluded by saying that he would know who was *with him* by observing who sacrificed to be there. If the Huskies were going to win, the extended team—the family, coaches, and friends—needed to commit as well.

When focusing on your goals, it is important for you to know who is in your support network and who is not. Ask your friends and family this: *Are you with me?*

If they are *with you*, then keep them on your team. If not, kick them off your squad. You will need to decide whether these unsupportive individuals should be placed on the sideline or completely removed from your life. The next chapter will cover how you should handle the people who are not *with you*.

> Coach's Rule: Know who is *with you* and who is not.

In football, once the ball is snapped, the quarterback runs the offense. He must read the coverage, implement the plays, make adjustments if necessary, and formulate quick decisions. The goal is to make forward progress. How he achieves this depends on the play. Perhaps he runs the ball, or hands it off to a halfback. Maybe he passes it to his star wide receiver. Regardless of the play, he needs ten other players on the field to be *with him*.

The chapter titled "What It Means to Win" will help you determine what your goals are. In "What's in Your Playbook," you'll define your plans for each of your objectives.

In life, you are the quarterback. You control the ball. But you'll need other players to be *with you*. A team of supporters is required to win. You must have wide receivers, running backs, and an offensive line.

The O-line is critical, but gets little glory. While they're not the *sexy* players shown on sports highlights, their role should not

be underestimated. The center, guards, and tackles use their size
and strength to protect the quarterback. They push the defensive
line back and clear paths for their teammates to break through
for a run. They're the foundation of the team's offense. A strong
offensive line helps win football games. A weak one can be catastrophic.

Jay Cutler experienced such
disastrous effects when he joined the
Chicago Bears in 2009. Plagued with
terrible pass protection, seven-step
drops, and slow-developing routes,
Cutler has been sacked 110 times in
forty-one games. This means Cutler often was on the run, trying to
dodge hungry pass rushers. A team
cannot win games if the offensive
line can't protect the quarterback.

Chicago Bears 2009–2011 seasons
✓ Have given up more sacks than any other team
✓ Have no offensive line-men ranked in the top 15 of any of the five O-line positions

The same is true in your personal life. You need an offensive
line to provide protection. Defenders will blitz, and you must also
beware of the blindside. Without the O-line and your other teammates, your chances of crossing the goal line are slim.

Winning was a habit for NFL-
coaching icon Vince Lombardi.
In his first season as head coach
with the Green Bay Packers, he
was named NFL Coach of the
Year. During his tenure with the

> *"The measure of who we are is what we do with what we have."*
> —Vince Lombardi

Packers, Lombardi led the team to five NFL championships in
seven years, three of which were consecutive wins. The Packers
became the first-ever Super Bowl champs in 1966. They then won
Super Bowl II the following year.

Lombardi was successful because he built upon the existing talent and reconditioned the team's mindset. He focused them on a winning mindset. With Vince, finishing second was not an option. Vince Lombardi knew what was needed to win.

> *"There is no room for second place. There is only one place in my game, and that's first place."*
> —Vince Lombardi

Look in the mirror, achieving your goals starts with you. First, you must believe in yourself. Second, you must commit to the game. Be obsessed with winning. Third, you must surround yourself with people who will help you win.

Do you have people that are currently *with you?* Will your existing team march alongside you toward your goal posts of victory? If so, build those people into your playbook. If not, drop them from your team.

As a teenager, one of my children struggled with depression and high levels of anxiety. As a coping mechanism, he resorted to self-mutilation. The act of cutting, scratching, or burning himself was an outlet to relive painful or hard-to-express feelings. It is not uncommon for adolescents to engage in this behavior. If left untreated, due to the individual's lack of self-control and the addictive nature of these acts, these behaviors can lead to actual suicide attempts. Unlike certain childhood behaviors, this was not something that my son would "grow out of." He needed professional help.

Our goal was to find a treatment plan that would help him better express his feelings, reduce his sense of loneliness, and increase his self-esteem. Having a team of supporters was critical in his ability to overcome this condition. He checked into a psychiatric hospital where he would be surrounded with a staff of professionals who were on his team. They, along with his psychologist, could provide him with coping tools and techniques necessary to achieve our goal. His family and friends were also *with him*—they provided emotional support and encouragement as my son went through this difficult time. Without this support network, the likelihood of achieving our goal would be very small. You must know who is *with you* and who will help you succeed.

Paul "Bear" Bryant is a college football coaching legend best known for his tenure as head coach at the University of Alabama. When Bryant retired in 1982, he held the record for most wins as a head coach in college football history: 323-85-17.

Bear Bryant had three rules for coaching:

Rule 1: *Surround yourself with people who can't live without football.*

Rule 2: *Recognize winners.*

Rule 3: *Have a plan for everything.*

Bear Bryant highlights:
✓ Led Crimson Tide to 6 national and 13 Southeastern Conference (SEC) championships
✓ During the 1960s and 1970s, no other team won more football games

This chapter focuses on the first two rules. The third rule is linked to developing your playbook, which is the underpinning needed to achieve your goals. Your plan will be discussed in later chapters.

"What Does It Mean to Win?" will help you identify your short-, medium-, and long-term goals. Once you define the goals, you must follow a three-step process.

COACH'S PLAYBOOK

1. Be committed to the goal.
2. Surround yourself with people who are passionate about your goals.
3. Know who the winners are on your team, and use them to get into the end zone.

Step 1: Are you committed to your goal? Are you with you?

You must be committed mentally, emotionally, and physically if you want to accomplish your goals. There are times when *you* won't be *with you.* Doubt and fear of the unknown and failure deter you from progressing forward. This critic within convinces us that we cannot achieve our dreams. It's a conservative inner voice who wants you to remain in your comfort zone. Push yourself into the *gray zone* and get comfortable with the unfamiliar. You *must eliminate the critic within.*

Step 2: Who shares your passion for this goal?

You need people who get excited about your ambitions. They may be people who aspire to achieve the same goal. They may simply be supporters committed to keeping you motivated. Let these friends know about your goals. Let your network's passion drive you to move forward. Use others to provide moral support and an attentive ear.

Next, let others know about it. You've already written down the goals, but now put it on the record. By making your support circle know what your goal is, you have increased your network of moral support and attentive ears. Learning from others can also accelerate your game plan. Your teammates will keep you grounded and energized to score.

I wanted to attend law school, but after graduating from engineering school, I could not afford to be a fulltime student. I was a single parent raising three children. I started working and put my law school plans on hold.

I revisited this goal five years later when I took a job with The Boeing Company. Boeing provided a generous educational benefit package, and I knew it was time to go back to school. One large constraint remained: *Who will watch my children while I'm in class?*

I called my mother, who was very supportive. She would watch the kids in the evenings. I started law school two months later. Attending evening classes three nights a week was tough. After my first year, I transferred to a more prestigious law school which required me to attend class four nights each week. It was almost unbearable. The support of my friends, employees, and coworkers kept me going. I used their energy to drive me forward. This is essential if you want to win.

While football and life have similarities, they also have differences. In football, the guys on the football field are *all* motivated to win the next game. Everything they do is focused on achieving this objective. On your life's field, not all of your teammates have to be driven towards your goal. Rather, most of your squad will have their own goals they are working towards. But these folks are willing to help you succeed in your life's goals as well. Find people who are passionate about seeing you achieve your dreams.

If you already have a support network in place, that is great. Keep them out on the field with you. If you do not have one, make it a priority to build your team. The first step is self-awareness. Identify what type of support structure you need. Then recruit your teammates.

Take an example of a mother who works full-time and wants to attend classes in the evening. She has children and will need coverage while she is in class. She considers the possibility of taking a class earlier in the day too. Now that she has identified these needs, she can look to see what family or friends might be willing to provide child care. She could also approach her boss to see if accommodations could be made with her work schedule to attend earlier classes.

No matter what situation you are in, this approach can work.

Step 3: Know who the winners are on your team.
Bear Bryant's second coaching rule was to recognize winners. You must have winners on your team. You need go-to receivers. A strong offensive line is essential. These players are going to protect you, but also energize you to press forward.

Shortly after I began writing this book, I attended a short writing course in Oklahoma City taught by New York *Times* best-selling author Bill Bernhardt. During the week-long class, my six fellow writers, our instructor, and I critiqued each other's work. While I learned valuable lessons about writing, the course gave me something that was priceless: *A group of winners who would motivate me every day to keep writing.*

When I walked in the room on the first day of class, I didn't know anyone. But when I left on Friday afternoon, I knew I had built new lifelong friendships. We kept in touch and created a private Facebook page where we posted every day. We supported each other and provided feedback on everyone's writing. My new teammates' passion and energy energized me. They kept me going by providing emotional support, allowing me to bounce ideas off them, and challenging my assertions. Thank you, Magnificent Seven (this is what our Facebook group is called)!

I worked fulltime while writing this book. I also had four children living at home. From Monday through Saturday each week, I shuffled kids between cheerleading practices, football games, fundraising activities, and other events. I easily could have made excuses for not writing. But I didn't because these winners were *with me*.

> Coach's Rule: You need winners on your team to energize you to complete your goals.

If you want to win your life's game, a team of supporters is required. Winning starts with defining your goals and having a plan, but you need a team to execute your playbook. Having winners on the field ensured that I would deliver. They helped me move the ball.

Knute Rockne was a phenomenal college football coach. As Notre Dame's head coach from 1918–1930, Rockne set what was, for many decades, the greatest all-time winning percentage record at 88.1 percent. He led Notre Dame to six national champion-

> *"The secret is to work less as individuals and more as a team. As a coach, I play not my eleven best, but my best eleven."*
> — Knute Rockne

ships and five undefeated seasons. Teamwork was the secret.

You have begun the journey with me down the field. Once you define your goals, you'll develop the playbook. You'll discover how to use your team to provide coverage, keep you grounded, and execute monumental plays. Put your best team forward and play the game with your winners. *Are you with me?*

Coach's Chalkboard

- Make sure you are with you.
- Find people that are with you.
- Identify winners to get into the end zone.

"I don't want ordinary people. I want people who are willing to sacrifice and do without a lot of those things ordinary students get to do. That's what it takes to win."

-Bear Bryant

Chapter 4:
Drop The Dead Weight

"If my mother put on a helmet and shoulder pads and a uniform that wasn't the same as the one I was wearing, I'd run over her if she was in my way. And I love my mother."—Bo Jackson

You must have people who are *with you*. But you must also recognize the ones who are not. Throughout your life, you'll encounter negative people who will argue and contradict you. In the office, we label coworkers who don't provide any value as *dead weight*.

The negative people in your life have the same effect. They provide no benefit on your life's field. You must *drop the dead weight*. Move them to the sideline, or remove them from your roster completely.

When identifying the dead weight in your personal life or in your career, do not make the mistake of giving someone this label simply because their view point differs from yours. In both the work and personal settings, you need diverse perspectives. It is a healthy way of doing business, in formulating the best approaches to solving problems, working on projects, and navigating through life. People that offer this different outlook are *not* dead weight. Generally, individuals that fall into this category are those that come to work only to collect a paycheck, are in "retirement mode", or are completely negative thinkers they are unproductive and unhealthy to the work organization and to your personal life. These individuals who fall into these categories provide no value. They will try to detract or distract you from achieving your goals. You cannot let these people get to you.

When I was a junior in college, my good friend told me he didn't think I would graduate. He never questioned my intelligence, but he felt it was too difficult for a teen single parent to complete a rigorous engineering program. *What the hell?*

I was stunned when I heard this. You can't control other's opinions or what they say to you, but you can choose how you react to the situation. I could have let his comment uninspire me and drag me down. Or I could ignore it and keep moving down the field.

I did the latter. While the obstacles were challenging, they weren't impossible. I worked my butt off and never lost sight of the end zone. My friend didn't intentionally try to hurt me; he thought he was doing the right thing in being honest. I appreciated his candidness, but benched him, and kept focused on my game. My friend apologized when I graduated.

> Coach's Rule: Do not let others' pessimism drag you down. Keep your eyes downfield and move the ball.

When I finished my undergraduate degree, I started working for the Department of Defense as a civilian engineer. I went to business school while working full time and earned a Masters of Business Administration (MBA). Similar to many other MBA graduates, I was ready to find a new position that used my business acumen.

I looked for work in the private sector. When I shared this with my parents, my father disagreed with my job search. He had grown up in an era where job stability was critical and people were loyal to one company. It was not uncommon to work for the same employer until retirement.

The younger generations had a different view. It was common to change companies multiple times in a person's career. If it provided career development and personal growth, I didn't mind switching employers.

My father was concerned that I was jeopardizing my financial stability and made his viewpoint known. Because dads have more life experience, they believe they know what is best for their children. Often times they are right. But sometimes young adults need to make choices on their own. If they fail, they must learn from the situation. If they succeed, they should be respected for making a smart decision.

My father was conservative when it came to managing his career. My philosophy was different. I was willing to take more risk. Even though I was a single mom with then three children, I considered all of my options. I had rainy-day money saved in the bank. In the event of a layoff, I had funds to sustain the family's lifestyle. At this time, I also had two engineering degrees and an MBA. This positioned me well. People with technical degrees combined with a business understanding were in high demand at that time. I was confident that I could find another job if I needed to.

My current job didn't align with my career aspiration of obtaining a senior management position in a large for-profit corporation. Since I was not moving the ball down the field, adjustments were in order. I was ready to move on. I ignored my father's comments and continued my job search. I received a tempting offer with Boeing for an engineering management position. I accepted the job and never looked back. I grew tremendously both personally and professionally from my first fulltime private industry position. A few months after working for Boeing, my father agreed that my decision was the right one.

In both examples, if I had listened to others, I could have walked down a different path—surely a road I would have regretted. I am passionate about living life the way I want to live it. I don't want to look back and say *I wish I had done that*.

Neither do you. Follow your dreams and just do it.

I never eliminated my friend or my father from my life. I simply kicked them off my football field and placed them on the sideline. My mom, on the other hand, remained on my field. She was an active supporter and was always willing to help me achieve my goals.

While it's okay to bench players, sometimes people don't even belong in your stadium. They must be removed from the game entirely.

When George Halas hired Mike Ditka as the Chicago Bears head coach for the 1982 season, Ditka warned his team turnover was in order. He said if the players were willing to work hard and stand with him, he promised a trip to the Super Bowl within the next three seasons. During his second season, the Bears went to the NFC Championship game but lost to San Francisco, who went on to win the Super Bowl.

Ditka's promise came true the following season when the Bears stomped on the New England Patriots 46–10 in Super Bowl XX. Ditka had eliminated the *dead weight* from the Bears. The resulting strong offense and elite defense won many games. During Ditka's eleven seasons as head coach, the Bears finished first in the NFC Central six times.

> Coach's Rule: Making forward progress requires moving players to the sideline or cutting them from the team.

Severing ties with players happens frequently. It's necessary to win. During the 2012 March Madness basketball tournament,

Kansas fans were fired up. I had a few friends watching the Final Four game between University of Kansas and Ohio State in my home theatre. Sports are exciting to follow on a high-definition, 138-inch projector screen.

The Kansas Jayhawks historically have been one of the most-storied programs in college basketball. Ohio State was also a basketball powerhouse. It was a close game throughout, but the Jayhawks pulled off a comeback win. Final score: Jayhawks 64, Buckeyes 62.

The Jayhawks basketball program was no stranger to victory and excellence. But the Kansas football team wasn't as successful, finishing last in the Big Twelve conference in the 2009, 2010, and 2011 seasons. Their conference record over these three seasons was a disappointing 2–23.

Kansas expected the 2012 season to be different. They signed former Notre Dame head coach Charlie Weis to make improvements. The first move Weis executed was to drop the dead weight. This resulted in a changed atmosphere with positive attitudes amongst those who remained.

> "The first change I made was to remove or dismiss several players who either didn't want to be a part of the program or acted in an inappropriate manner."
> —Charlie Weis, *USA Today*

The Jayhawks only won five games over the 2010 and 2011 seasons. None were conference wins. Nobody expected the Jayhawks to make a major bowl appearance in 2012, but fans expected better team performance. Winning for the Jayhawks would be to get a Big-Twelve conference victory. Cutting unfocused team members was critical. Though the Jayhawks did not achieve a Big-Twelve win during the 2012 season, by dropping the dead weight, Kansas has completed the first step to succeeding. The next step for 2013 will be to focus on their playbook. The same is true in your life. Once you have built your team of supporters and eliminated the non-value added players, you are ready to focus on developing your game-winning strategies. Similar to the Kansas Jayhawks, sometimes winning will not occur during the first year. It could take more time. "Keep Your Head in the Game" details the need for patience in life when trying to achieve your goals.

While Kansas is still working towards winning, one college team that had successfully cut team members and executed their playbook was Steve Spurrier's University of South Carolina Gamecocks. The 2005 season was Spurrier's first season as the Gamecocks' head coach. While many did not expect the Gamecocks to have a winning season, the team pulled off a five-game Southeastern Conference (SEC) winning streak, for their first time in their SEC history. The *Associated Press* named Spurrier SEC Coach of the Year and the Gamecocks earned a trip to the Independence Bowl. The following season, Spurrier led the Gamecocks to the Liberty Bowl where they beat the University of Houston Cougars. Spurrier became the first head coach in University of South Carolina history to take a football team to two bowl games during his first two years as a head coach. Steve Spurrier built a team of winners and cut those who were not. You must do the same in life.

On your life's field, there are people who will detract from you or distract you. You cannot let these individuals stop you from getting into the end zone. You must remain committed to your goal; don't stop until you reach it.

Coach's Chalkboard

1. You cannot control other people's viewpoints, but you can control how you respond to them.

2. Keep the players who are with you.

3. Drop the ones who are not.

Chapter 5:
What Does It Mean To Win?

"Set your goals high, and don't stop 'til you get there."—Bo Jackson

Winning is important. Whether it's in football or in life, each victory energizes players to push forward. It fuels us to want to win again.

In every football game, the team understands the definition of winning. *They must put more points on the board than their opponents.* This objective focuses players on the short-term horizon. But football encompasses more than a single game's performance. Similar to life, football teams must have short-, medium-, and long-term goals. The *short* and the *medium* are focused on the tactical, while the *long* concentrates on the strategic.

A football team's perspective on winning extends past a single season. For every team, the short-term goal is to win football games. Beyond that, it differs. A medium-term goal could be to make the playoffs. The longer-term focus might be on building a team to win a BCS national championship or play in a bowl game. Each of these goals will depend on the team's situation and will require different playbooks to achieve.

Goals are important because they define where you want to go. The journey down your life's field is meaningless if you do not know where you are going. You must know what winning means to you. It's defined differently by everyone. Make time to think through this. Before you set foot on your football field ready to play the game, you must have identified your goals. Similar to leading a football team or running a business, you must answer three questions:

ASK YOURSELF THE FOLLOWING:

1. Who am I?

2. Where do I want to go?

3. How am I going to get there?

Step 1: What do you stand for? What is your vision?

It's important to know what your core values are. Understanding who you are and what you stand for is a defining moment. Ask, *Who Am I?* Spend as much time as you need to answer this question—it's a critical one. Once you have the answer, write it down. Then develop your personal vision statement. Your vision will provide direction on what winning means to you. It will help you chart the course in both your personal life and your career.

Some questions to help you define your vision are:
- What are my top five values?
- What is important in my life?
- What do you enjoy?
- What excites and energizes you?

Take a high school teacher, Jim, as an example. Some of Jim's top values are integrity and treating people with respect. Jim wants to make an impact in the lives of young adults. As a middle-aged man with no children, he finds being around teenagers very rewarding and would like to do more. Jim has a good idea of who he is, and is ready to move to Step 2.

Step 2: What do you want in life?

Often times, we focus on what other people expect of us. We concentrate on delivering what they want. Now is the time to think about you. Look at your vision statement. What do you want? What are your dreams and ambitions? Write them down. Think about all aspects of life—spiritual, career, physical, family, financial and more. Be sure to include goals that address all three time horizons: short-term (1–2 years), medium-term (3–5 years), and long-term (5+ years). Reach far and set high expectations for yourself.

In the case of Jim, he is content with his career. But he feels like he should be more involved with youth groups. Some of Jim's goals could be:

> **Short-term:** *By the end of next year, become a volunteer twice a week at the local community center.*
>
> **Medium-term:** *Save $30,000 over the next five years to start a non-profit organization designed at providing programs and services for at-risk teenagers.*
>
> **Long-term:** *Within the next seven years, establish my non-profit organization, build volunteer staff to ten members, and have three outreach programs in place.*

Step 3: How will you achieve them?

The first two steps defined you and your goals. They focused on the *who* and the *what*. This step focuses on the *how*. What is your plan to accomplish what you want? The chapter, "What's in Your Playbook" will help you answer this.

Congratulations. You now have a list of what you want. But there is still more work to do. Ask yourself if your goals are specific and achievable. Do they capture what you really want and what you think is important? Put each goal through the SMART test. If one or more fail, revise them until they pass.

S	=	Specific (I have sufficient detail)
M	=	Measurable (I can measure it)
A	=	Actionable (I can do something about it)
R	=	Relevant (I am aligned with this goal)
T	=	Time-bound (I have a set timeframe)

Examples of SMART goals would be 1) *I want to lose twenty pounds in three months* and 2) *I want to complete my master's degree in business within the next four years.*

Now that your goals have passed the SMART test, take another hard look at them. Ask yourself again, *Is this what I want?* Are your head, your heart, and your guts aligned with these goals? As the quarterback on your life's field, you are the leader. You own the ball and will work with your team to move it forward. You create your future, so make sure these goals reflect what you want.

The game of life is remarkable because it's dynamic. Circumstances on the field will drive you to play differently. Sometimes, your desires will change. The list you have defined today may not be what you want tomorrow. You must periodically evaluate your goals to determine whether they're still valid. If they're not, you'll need to revisit the goal-setting process.

As the starting quarterback at Edmond Santa Fe High School, Brandon Weeden was on the path to a successful football career. He led his team to win the Oklahoma State High School semifinals—the school's first ever playoff appearance. He later was named MVP and Offensive Player of the Year. Weeden also excelled off the football field, in sports such as baseball and basketball.

He was drafted to play Major League Baseball for the New York Yankees and bounced around, eventually landing with a minor league team. After years in the minors and riddled with injuries, Weeden quit baseball. He reevaluated his goals and enrolled at Oklahoma State University. Now he was focused on football.

In 2009, Weeden led the Cowboys to an eleven-point comeback victory over the University of Colorado in a nationally televised game. In 2011, he led Oklahoma State to an 11–1 regular season, where they ranked third in the BCS standings. The Cowboys went on to win the Tostitos Fiesta Bowl that year.

Weeden had recognized that due to limitations he needed a change from baseball and wanted to play professional football. The first step was performing at the college level. His strong performances created the ideal opportunity and Weeden was drafted by the Cleveland Browns in 2012. Refocusing his goals worked for Weeden. He played the game and had won.

The takeaway from Weeden's story is that it is okay to reevaluate and adjust your goals. Weeden initially focused on baseball, but due to injuries and lack-luster seasons, he decided to make a change and pursue a different goal. In life we have to consider our limitations when defining our goals. At five-foot two, my chances of playing professional basketball are pretty slim.

While I love playing basketball almost as much as football, I have no plans to pursue a Women's National Basketball Association (WNBA) career. It is not a fit for me, and I am okay with that.

Remember, you have one life so make sure you are happy along the way. We are human beings, not human *doings.* Before we enter life's field and start to *do,* we need to know who we are, so we can focus our actions to align with what we want. Defining your vision statement is the first step in this process. Next, you must set goals that align with your being. You must commit to your goals and develop a strategy to get into the end zone. You are now ready to build your playbook.

Coach's Chalkboard

1. Define who you are before you play the game.

2. Set goals to provide direction for your life.

3. Stretch yourself by setting your goals high.

4. Commit yourself to winning.

5. Revisit your goals to make sure they are still valid. If they aren't, then develop new ones.

Chapter 6:

What's In Your Playbook?

"If you can believe it, the mind can achieve it."—Ronnie Lott

Every football team wants to win. The playbook plays a critical part in achieving the victory. Similar to football, you *must* have a playbook to win life's game.

Tom Landry was the head coach of the Dallas Cowboys for twenty-nine years. During his tenure, he led the Cowboys to two Super Bowl championships in 1972 and 1978. Landry is currently third on the NFL all-time winning list with 270 wins. He had a strong playbook.

> *"Setting a goal is not the main thing. It is deciding how you will go about achieving it and staying with that plan."*
> —Tom Landry

Every great football coach knows how important the playbook is to winning. "Are You With Me?" introduced Bear Bryant's three rules of coaching. His third rule focused on the playbook: *Have a plan for everything.*

Defining your goals is an important first step. However, if you don't have a game-winning strategy, then defining the goal is of no value. You need a plan.

"What Does it Mean to Win?" introduced three strategic questions for you to answer. The first two focused on defining your goals—what it meant to win. The third question involves building your plan to achieve those goals.

BUILDING THE PLAYER'S PLAYBOOK

1. Has the game started? Is it still the pre-game?

2. Where are you on your football field?

3. Who are the defenders?

4. Who is with you?

5. Where is the dead weight?

6. Who is your competition? (for career-related goals)

7. Are you committed to the goal?

Step 1: Are you already playing the game?

You are currently pursuing your short-term goals. Others are future-focused. When building your playbook, your present-day goals will have a different plan than the longer-term ones. While a plan is needed for every goal, you should devote more of your energy developing and executing your playbook for these shorter-term goals. The time frame you have set to accomplish these goals is less than your future focused goals. Since these goals are ones that are one to two years out, you should already be playing the game or getting ready to play the game. The next step is being aware of how far you need to move the ball to get into the end zone.

Step 2: What's your field position?

You need to know where you presently are on the field. Have you started working on your goal? If so, evaluate how much progress you have made. This will shape your action plan. Consider your field position and what strategies you need in order to cross the goal line. If you are inside the twenty, congratulations—you are in the red zone. You need a near-term focused playbook that you can execute with speed and accuracy. If you haven't begun to pursue the goal, then you are at your own two-yard line. You'll need plays that can move the ball the entire field and get you into the end zone.

Step 3: Who are the defenders?

You must be aware of who is in your stadium. You now know how to distinguish your teammates from dead weight. Your teammates are on your side and you've dropped the non-value added players. Now it's time to address your opponents, which can be both people and circumstances. These defenders are the obstacles in your life. Their sole purpose is to limit your forward progress. Know who and what stands in between you and the first-down marker. Anticipate their moves and develop strong plays around them. Identify what tactics you can incorporate to move the ball forward.

Take a look at Wanda. Her goal is getting her undergraduate degree. Her opponent is a lack of money. She will need to identify a plan that allows her to eliminate or minimize this defender. Some tactics she can explore are 1) applying for financial aid,

2) a personal loan, or 3) attending a community college for the first couple of years to minimize education expenses.

No matter what the situation is, once you know your field position, you must be aware of all defenders on the field. Then you can build strategies into your playbook to overcome them. Think creatively when developing your plans and stretch yourself beyond your comfort zone. Sometimes you need to get comfortable with the uncomfortable if you want to win. Learn to navigate in that unfamiliar *gray zone.*

Step 4: Who will support you?

"Are You with Me?" focused on teamwork and your support network. Evaluate who is *with you,* and build these people into your playbook.

Step 5: Who will distract you?

There are people in your life that do not support your goals. While someone may support one goal, he may not support another. You must be aware of who will distract or detract you from achieving your goals. Drop this *dead weight* from your playbook by either kicking them to the sideline or completely severing your ties.

Step 6: Who is your competition?

Playing the career game involves being aware of your competition. You must know who and what your opponents' strengths are. You need to anticipate their moves, and develop a playbook that positions you to beat them. In business, understanding the competitive landscape is critical; moving your career forward requires the same. You must have a plan that differentiates you from others. You need a brand that is unique to you and provides value to your current company, as well as prospective employers. "Play like a Free Agent" will expand on personal branding. Make sure you understand your competition. Then include plays in your playbook that help you develop your brand and beat out your competitors.

Step 7: Are you committed to winning?

Great athletes and coaches mentally, physically, and emotionally commit to the game. For them, winning is the only option. They believe in themselves and build a playbook that positions them to win.

Ronnie Lott is widely known as one of the best defensive backs in NFL history. He is recognized as one of the greatest seventy-five NFL players and was a member of both the 1980 and 1990 NFL All-Decade Teams. Lott knew the importance of believing, which was key to his success.

> *"If you believe in yourself and have dedication and pride - and never quit, you'll be a winner. The price of victory is high but so are the rewards."*
> —Bear Bryant

You *too* must be fixated on winning. You need to get in your zone to develop and execute your plan. Believe in yourself and be creative in your playbook. Develop actions that break the rules of normality. Be innovative and find a way to win.

Coach's Chalkboard

- A strong playbook is essential to winning.
- Understand who is on the field with you.
- Leverage your team.
- Drop the dead weight.
- Believe in yourself.
- Be creative in developing your action plan.
- Commit to winning.

Chapter 7:

Check Your Ego Both On And Off The Field

"The principle is competing against yourself. It's about self-improvement, about being better than you were the day before. "—Steve Young

In football, there are athletes and then there are great athletes. Without a doubt, both groups are skilled; talent is not the differentiator. Rather, something more powerful separates the two. Truly elite athletes exhibit a professional attitude while keeping their egos in check. All others fall short. While some athletes and coaches boast impressive stats, without the right attitude, those individuals have never *really* achieved greatness.

Performance alone can make someone good, but proper character is essential to be great. People admire players who are refined. Fans cheer them on and want them to succeed. On the other hand, *no one* likes the prima donna. While hotshots can capitalize and make the immediate moment exciting, over the long term, the feeling is different. Playing alongside them is frustrating. Watching how they carry themselves is embarrassing.

"Are You With Me?" focused on the criticality of teamwork in both football and life. It's important for you to surround yourself with a group of supporters who will keep you grounded and help you move the ball forward. Your attitude both on and off the field will determine who *wants* to be *with you*. It's a necessary component to recruiting and keeping winners on your squad.

Everyone respects the player with class and character. These individuals energize their team and focus on making *the team* successful. This is who you want to be. These players' charismatic attitude extends beyond the game. Both on and off the field, their personality remains the same.

This isn't unique to football. In business, the same holds true. No one likes working with the guy who continually brags about how great he is. You know these people. You also know people who are humble, unselfish, and who care about others. These are the people who are inspiring; others would follow them anywhere.

KEEPING YOUR EGO IN CHECK

1. Do not be the prima donna

2. Play the game with class

3. Keep a positive attitude

4. Never think you are good enough

Your playbook should be as sacred to you as it is to a football team. A strong strategy provides an advantage over your opponents. You need that edge. However, if you don't have a strong team to help execute the plays, then your plan is worthless. You need to play like a great athlete and hold your ego in check both on and off the field. Whether you are aggressively working toward a goal or taking a time-out, the way you carry yourself must not change. People observe you in all circumstances. They remember how you behave, and it shapes their impression of you. Make sure you're displaying the qualities you expect winners to exhibit. If you do, your network of supporters will be vast, and you'll progress forward. Remember the following four rules to keep your ego in check.

Rule #1: Check your ego—Lose the superstar mentality

The prima donna mentality is everywhere. From business to sports to life, it exists. Do not let it creep into your stadium. While you should be proud of your accomplishments, you can do that without acting like a superstar. People will recognize your contributions without your self-promotion. Bragging and acting like *you are better than the rest* is a turnoff. You must avoid doing this.

Football players like Terrell Owens and Chad Johnson (formerly Chad Ochocinco) have made their mark on the NFL. Coaches, players, and spectators all agree that these two athletes *had game*. But where are they now? They aren't playing professional football. No team wanted to pick them up for the 2012 season. Their shenanigans and lack of a professional attitude contributed to this outcome.

Contrast these players to those like running back Adrian Peterson, quarterback Payton Manning, and defensive end Dwight Freeney. These three are the highest-salaried NFL athletes for their respective positions. While their pocketbook and their talent level rose to superstardom, their egos haven't followed suit. They don't act like megastars. Fans and fellow teammates love them. These athletes play the game with professionalism and promote an environment where others want to be around them. They're humble and don't act like they're better than the rest. Learn from these great players, and don't get big-headed.

Rule #2: Check yourself—Don't be a dirty player

While playing football at the University of Nebraska, defensive tackle Ndamukong Suh gained a reputation as being an aggressive player. This intensified when he began his professional football career with the Detroit Lions. In one of his first preseason games, Suh grabbed Cleveland Browns quarterback Jake Delhomme by the facemask and threw him to the ground. Although his opponent was not hurt, Suh was fined $7,500 for this incident.

As a rookie in the NFL, he should have learned from this event and refrained from repeating it. Suh didn't care and remained a dirty player. The following season, he was ejected from the game after he stomped on the arm of Evan Dietrich-Smith, a back-up guard for the Green Bay Packers. This resulted in a three-game suspension for Suh. Similar to the fine, this penalty didn't deter him from his dirty tactics. The next season he kicked quarterback Matt Ryan in the groin. He has continued to take shots that most other players would avoid. That's not how the game of football should be played. The game is not about winning at all costs.

The NFL's focus on player safety reaffirms this position. The game should be won by playing fairly and not trying to hurt other players. Winners should come out on top because they played the game better that day and played it cleanly. The same is true in life.

As the quarterback in your life's game, don't play dirty. Whether you're on the field or are taking a time-out, you must act the same way in either situation. Look at those who have inspired you. How do they treat others? Remember, it takes a team if you want to win. People observe you in all circumstances and form impressions. If you engage in questionable behaviors, you'll quickly lose your supporters. There is also a difference between playing dirty and being driven. You can be motivated and hard-charging, but still treat others with respect. Never intentionally hurt anyone.

> *"Show class, have pride, and display character. If you do, winning takes care of itself."*
> —Bear Bryant

Atlanta Falcons tight end Tony Gonzales is a prime example of an athlete with character both on and off the field. He has a reputation for compassion and cares about more than himself. While he has been building a Hall-of-Fame career in the NFL, he also supports other worthy causes through the Tony Gonzales Foundation. His involvement is not limited to monetary contributions. Shadow Buddies is a program that makes dolls to comfort and educate sick kids and their families. Since Gonzales' involvement with Shadow Buddies, he has delivered over 21,000 dolls to children. His clean personality exists both in and out of the stadium. It doesn't change. You must live your life like Tony Gonzales and play your game with class. That is how real winners beat the game and how you should too.

Rule #3: Check your attitude—always maintain a positive outlook, inspire others, and treat people with respect

How do you feel when a grumpy, negative person walks in the room? It drags down not only your drive, but those around you as well. Conversely, when you interact with an optimistic, cheerful person, it energizes you and is refreshing. You are motivated to get things done when you are surrounded by people like this. If you want to be successful, you need to display a positive attitude.

> Coach's Rule: If you step onto the field negative, then you won't do as well if you go in with a positive outlook.

Remember, teammates are essential if you want to achieve your goals. Besides having a confident and upbeat personality, you must treat your fellow players with respect. Without it, they won't execute your playbook, and your forward progress will be severely hampered. With it, your chances of getting in the end zone increase drastically.

The *USS Benfold* is a powerful, 8,600-ton ship in the US Navy's fleet of guided-missile destroyers. Years ago it was in serious trouble. When Capt. D. Michael Abrashoff assumed command, operations were dysfunctional, and the *Benfold's* reenlistment rate was only twenty-eight percent.

In the span of twenty months, he and his crew turned the *Benfold* around. It became the best-performing ship in the US Pacific Fleet. The *Benfold* won a trophy as the most combat-ready ship in the fleet. The ship's retention rate also improved to one-hundred percent. In Abrashoff's book *It's Your Ship, Management Techniques from the Best Damn Ship in the Navy,* he explains sailors left because they felt they were not being treated with respect and dignity. He changed the culture

> *"Leaders need to understand how profoundly they affect people, how their optimism and pessimism are equally infectious, how directly they set the tone and spirit of everyone around them."*
> —Capt D. Michael Abrashoff (ret.)

and gave his men the respect they deserved and should have received all along. This made the difference, and his accomplishments were exceptional.

When playing life's game you must also inspire others. Indianapolis Colt's Chuck Pagano is one who sets this example. In 2012, this first-time head coach was diagnosed with acute promyelocytic leukemia, which is a cancer of the blood and bone marrow. Though facing the battle for his life and undergoing rigorous chemotherapy treatments, Pagano never lost his warm attitude and positive outlook.

The Colts finished the previous season with the worst record in the NFL. Chuck's display of courage and optimism with his battle fueled the team to turn things around on the field. The Colts played every game with unyielding heart, and their performances have been incredible. While their head coach sat watching games from afar in his hospital bed, the Colts won games no one thought possible.

The Colts' support for Pagano extended beyond the football game. Almost three-dozen Colts team members and two cheerleaders shaved their heads in honor of Pagano. The community also got involved. Covenant Christian High School football players followed suit and shaved their heads, too. Additionally, over a quarter-million dollars was raised for leukemia research through CHUCKSTRONG bracelet and t-shirt sales. Pagano's attitude has been infectious and has sparked incredible support for finding a cure for leukemia.

You don't have to be famous to positively affect others. Anyone can do it. Consider, for example, Mason Harvey, an obese twelve-year-old boy from Oklahoma City. Over twelve million children in the United States today are obese and are at risk for serious health problems down the road. Mason was headed down that path. In sixth grade, he weighed 206 pounds and was bullied because he was overweight. Mason was determined to make a change.

He altered his diet and began working out. His hard work paid off and he dropped eighty-five pounds. Mason didn't stop there. Not only did he encourage his parents to adopt a healthier lifestyle, he organized fitness events to increase awareness of childhood obesity. His drive inspired his friends to eat healthier as well. Mason Harvey is a young boy who truly is an inspiration.

A great player, both in football and in life, energizes others. Be like Mason Harvey. Be like Chuck Pagano. Inspire your teammates and their response will be overwhelming.

Rule #4: Check your awareness—focus on how you can improve

One big mistake athletes and individuals make is assuming that they are good enough. They feel entitled and are disgruntled when what they want in life is not handed to them. Winning life's game involves hard work. You do

> *"Doing the same thing over and over again and expecting different results."*
> —Albert Einstein's definition of insanity

not achieve your goals without continuous improvement. If you want to get into the end zone, you cannot use the same practices that got you where you are today. You must make changes and adopt new plays. Look inside yourself and make the commitment today to change.

Self-awareness is an important part of your playbook. You must be aware of what is and is not working for you. What is prohibiting you from moving the ball forward? Where can you improve? Spend some time flushing this out.

Great players know what their gaps are and train every day to make advancements. Even when it seems like they have reached their peak, they strive for more. Running back Adrian Peterson has consistently rushed for 1,000-plus-yard seasons (except for 2011, when he reached 970 yards before suffering a season-ending injury). While many would be content with this level of performance, it wasn't good enough for Peterson. He wanted a 2,000-yard season, a feat accomplished by only six others in the NFL.

In 2012, Peterson led the league in rushing yards. With his speed, flexibility, and athleticism, his goal was certainly attainable. In December 2012, Peterson reached his goal becoming the seventh running back to eclipse a 2000-yard season. He even came nine yards short of beating Eric Dickerson's NFL record of 2,105 yards in a single season. Key to achieving this goal was Peterson's self-improvement mentality. He trained relentlessly and strived to achieve a higher-level of greatness.

Tony Dorsett was another elite athlete, thought of as one of the greatest running backs in college football history. As a four-time All-American, he finished his college career with 6,082 total rushing yards, an NCAA record (later surpassed by Ricky Williams in 1998). He was passionate about

> *"To succeed... You need to find something to hold on to, something to motivate you, something to inspire you."*
> —Tony Dorsett

football and used his love for the game to excel both on and off the field. It inspired him to achieve greatness in football and in life. Like Dorsett and Peterson, you must find something to motivate you.

What drives you to want to win? Use that to inspire you and spend time each day focusing on self-improvement. Do not settle for where you are today. Don't be ordinary, strive to be extraordinary.

This chapter focused on four important aspects around your attitude: First, no one likes the prima donna. Everyone respects the unpretentious player. In life, you will need supporters to help you achieve your goals. Rather it is providing emotional support, financial support, or helping you make a connection, individuals will be more willing to be on your team if you are humble. Second, you cannot play life the dirty way. Be a classy character both on and off the field. Third, a great athlete has a positive mindset. This optimistic outlook strengthens the ability to execute. It drives teammates to want to move the ball forward. Fourth, you cannot settle for your current level of performance. Focus on self-improvement.

If you want to win in life, you must treat your supporters with consideration and respect. If you don't, you'll lose your teammates quickly. Remain positive, be humble, and inspire others. It's your ticket to getting into the end zone.

Coach's Chalkboard

- A professional attitude separates the great athletes from the good and the mediocre.
- Keep your ego in check both on and off the field.
- A positive outlook will go much farther than a negative one.
- Don't settle for who you are today; focus on self-improvement, and achieve greatness tomorrow.

Chapter 8:
Move the ball

"A good back makes his own holes. Anybody can run where the holes are."
—Joe Don Looney

In football, size matters. So does speed, agility, flexibility, and the ability to scramble. Yes, stats matter, too. Life is no different. But your physical size is not the driving force to get you in the end zone; rather, it's the size and strength of your determination. Move at a pace that aligns with your goals. Your short-term goals might require a more intense focus over the next six months, while you can work at a slower pace on the long-term goals. Keep in mind your playbook will require adjustments, and you must be flexible in your plan. Your track record—your ability to execute—is most critical.

If you want to win the game, you need to progress the ball down the field. You must cross the goal line and score. While some football teams rely on a strong defense to score points-off-turnovers that is not the normal way to play the game. When the Chicago Bears' offense collapses, the strong defense comes to the rescue. It works for them, but don't play life's game that way. The defense is supposed to prevent the opponent from getting into the end zone, but it's the offense that must drive the score-board.

Oklahoma University quarterback Landry Jones has been followed closely. The 2011 game against Kansas State was unforgettable. Jones threw for an OU record-setting 505 yards and five touchdowns. That night, K-State and OU fans watched as the Sooners proved they could move the ball. Final score: Oklahoma 58, Kansas State 17. The offense dominated; they drove the win.

The same is true on your life's football field. Without offensive forward progress your chances of succeeding are limited. You might get lucky and still score, but in most cases, you need to proactively move the ball forward. You must use your teammates, the people who are *with you*, to drive into the end zone.

"Are You with Me?" highlighted the need for different players on your football team. In life's game, you are the quarterback. But your game requires a team to get first downs. The Oklahoma Sooners pummeled the Kansas State Wildcats because the offensive line owned the line of scrimmage. The offen-sive tackles prevented K-State from blitzing and blindsiding the quarterback. The O-line stopped the defense from sacking Jones, allowing him enough time to canvas the field, drop back, and connect with his wide receivers.

> **2011 NCAA Div. 1A Stats**
>
> ✓ **Landry Jones of Oklahoma:** 355 out of 362 passing for 4,463 yards and 29 TDs
>
> ✓ **Matt Barkley of USC:** 39 TDs in a single season, a USC record; 468 yards in a single game, also a USC record
>
> ✓ **Denard Robinson of Michigan:** 142 out of 258 passing for 2,173 yards and 20 TDs; 221 carries for 1,176 yards and 16 TDs
>
> ✓ **Trent Richardson of Alabama:** 283 carries, 1,679 yards, 21 TDs

"What Does It Mean to Win" identified the need to define your goals. "What's in Your Playbook" then provided guidance on building your strategies to achieve each goal. The set of plays in your playbook becomes your action plan. It's a critical component that you'll need to win.

Once you define your playbook, you must execute it. Making the action plan is an easier step. Implementing it can be more difficult. It requires changing your behaviors. This can be challenging because you have developed habits over time. You are in a rhythm with your day-to-day, weekly, and monthly activities.

Now it's time for change. Getting out of your normal routine requires stretching beyond your comfort zone. Let's face it. If playing life's game was easy, everyone would win it. You'll need to make sacrifices. You may have to shift priorities. It starts with making choices, sometimes difficult ones.

As the quarterback, you are in control and must make decisions that will move the ball forward. Great athletes know the importance of sacrifice and change their lifestyle because they're committed to the goal. Get out of your comfort space. If you are not willing to do that, then you run the risk of keeping the same field position. Don't be scoreless on the field, heading down a winless path.

We stretch our kids because we believe their potential allows for more. It's time for you to do the same. Believe in yourself and press forward. At the end of each week, ask yourself:

What did I do to move the ball?
Did I make forward progress?
How do I advance the ball?
What holes can I create to move the ball?
How can I get my next first down?

In business, football, and life, the winners know how to complete their action plans. They assess their field position, evaluate their playbook, and choose the right plays to advance the ball. They also use their teammates to move forward. You must do the same. No matter how great the obstacles, you must implement your playbook. Don't be afraid to stand out from the ordinary. Great athletes excel because they push themselves to be extraordinary.

The Heisman trophy is the most prestigious college football award, created to recognize the *best of the best*—the MVP of the college football season. Typically, the top Heisman candidates are quarterbacks and running backs. While a wide receiver sometimes wins this distinguished honor, only two have won in the past twenty-five years.

The Heisman is awarded through public voting. One reason contenders get votes is because they can execute the plays when it matters most. The only fulltime defensive player to ever win the Heisman was former University of Michigan defensive back Charles Woodson. Known for his spectacular play making, he received almost three hundred more voting points than the runner-up, University of Tennessee quarterback Peyton Manning.

> **Recent Heisman Trophy Winners**
> - ✓ QB Robert Griffin III, Baylor University
> - ✓ QB Cam Newton, Auburn University
> - ✓ RB Mark Ingram, University of Alabama

Woodson won this award because of memorable plays such as the one-handed sideline interception against rival Michigan State. Woodson also led the Wolverines to an undefeated season and a national championship. He proves that anyone can be an MVP. He strove for excellence and proved himself worthy of the Heisman. Today, Woodson continues to shine as a defensive back for the Green Bay Packers.

In your personal life, you need to be the MVP. No matter what the obstacles, you must rise above them. You must stay focused on winning and execute the playbook. If no one has ever accomplished what you are seeking to achieve, do not be intimidated. Charles Woodson did it with the Heisman; you can do it too.

In your career, you want to be recognized as the go-to guy (or gal). One piece of advice many executives and officers of *Fortune* 50 companies have told me is, *Focus on performing in the job you have.*

While it's important to plan ahead, you cannot lose sight of executing in your current role. I have seen many coworkers so focused on their next job that they neglect their current responsibilities and fail to perform in their present position. If people recognize you as someone who can do the job, they will help you advance your career. Wins today help position you for wins tomorrow.

Urban Meyer is a head coach with an impressive record of turning around and improving teams. He started his head coaching career with Bowling Green State University, who had finished the previous football season with a record of 2–9. In his first year, Meyer and the Falcons finished the season with an 8–3 record.

Two seasons later, he left to head coach the Utah Utes, another struggling football team who finished the previous year

> The Florida Gators were the first football program to win two BCS Championship games under the same coach, Coach Urban Meyer.

with a 5–6 record. Meyer and the team went 10–2 in the first year. The next year they went undefeated. After Utah, he went to head coach for the Florida Gators, improving their season to 9–5 during his first year. The following season, the Gators beat Ohio State in the BCS National Championship 41–14. Two years later, Meyer with quarterback Tim Teebow beat out the Oklahoma

Sooners in the BCS National Championship 24–14. With every coaching job he took, Urban Meyer focused on performing in his current job. His leadership and commitment to his team proves why he was Ohio State's number-one choice as the Buckeye's head coach for the 2012 football season.

People also excel in their career when they provide additional value to the organization. This is done by taking on additional projects to fill the gaps. Organizations know what their holes are and seek out players who can fill them. Be willing to help out the larger organization when your skills are a fit. People recognize winners who help them win. Your commitment to their goals can lead to promising career opportunities for you.

However, one word of caution: *Know your limits! Do not overcommit.* When you volunteer for too many projects, you run the risk of not succeeding in the extra work or your normal responsibilities. You must remain focused on your day-to-day commitments and volunteer for extra work as your workload allows.

Things never go as planned all the time. Be sure to make necessary adjustments to your playbook when needed. Coaches know the importance of adjustments. They monitor the team's ability to execute and make adjustments when their current strategy is not working. You must do the same when playing your life's game.

The goal of a football game is to win. That goal doesn't change. Your life is a little different. When assessing your field position, be sure to reevaluate your goals. People change, circumstances change, and your desires change. Brandon Weeden started off trying to play major league baseball. Due to limitations such as injuries, he modified his goals and is now focused on a professional football career. You too must decide if it's time to make a change.

If your goal is still important, then assess your field position. Make adjustments to your playbook. Develop new plays and execute them.

On life's football field, you have defined what it means to win and decided what needs to happen. You control whether you'll get the next first down. You know what it takes to score and have developed your playbook. You have people who are *with you*. Now it's time to execute. Congratulations! You are now ready to move the ball.

Coach's Chalkboard

1. Define your playbook and execute it.

2. Be the MVP and make plays when it matters most.

3. Just because it has not been done before is no excuse why you cannot achieve a goal.

4. In your career, focus on executing in your current job.

5. Volunteer to help others, but do not overcommit.

6. Make adjustments when necessary.

7. You must drive the ball forward. You are in control.

Chapter 9:

Get The Next First Down

"Without self-discipline, success is impossible, period."—Lou Holtz

You are on the football field and control the ball. You have your playbook and are ready to execute. Now you must get your next first down. Look downfield. Where is the first-down marker? How will you know when you have reached it?

In football, the answer is simple. Assuming no offensive penalties, the team must advance the ball at least ten yards to get the next first down. On your life's field, the first-down marker is not as obvious.

You have defined short-, medium-, and long-term goals. For each of these goals, you must identify milestones. These are your checkpoints. These indicators will help you measure your field position and ball movement.

Once these milestones have been established, you must keep your eyes on the first down marker and have self-discipline to get there. Make the commitment today to get the next first down. Use your teammates to implement the playbook and move the ball forward.

> Coach's Rule: Keep focused on your next milestone and have the self-discipline to get the next first down.

Radio executive George Richards brought the Lions football team to Michigan in 1934, where the team placed second in the Western Division. The following season, George "Potsy" Clark led the Lions to their first NFL Championship. With a World Series victory and an NFL title championship occurring a few months apart, Michiganders saw a glimmer of hope during the Great Depression.

However, the silver lining didn't last for long, and the Lions struggled throughout the next decade. The 1950s proved better when the Lions won back-to-back NFL championships. But as swiftly as the glory days came, they also went. The arrival of Barry Sanders in 1989 sparked new momentum, but that too would soon fade. Their losing streak continued into the new millennium and hit the bottom with a winless season in 2008.

Since the NFL North's inception in 2002, Detroit had consistently placed in the bottom two slots of the division standings, but this changed in 2011. They won their first two games. In Week 3, the Lions then came back from a 20-point deficit to beat the Minnesota Vikings 26–23. They continued to shine, beating the Dallas Cowboys and the Chicago Bears in the following two games. The Lions were roaring loudly with a 5–0 season start. They stunned football fans by completing the season with a 10–6 record.

The Lion's self-discipline, commitment to getting first downs, and focus on winning games earned them a playoff spot. Michiganders were elated. For years, they had waited for this moment. In January 2012, the Lions played the New Orleans Saints in the wildcard playoff game. This was the team's opportunity to prove themselves in the postseason.

The Lions started off strong, playing like playoff veterans, but they eventually wore down. Quarterback Drew Brees and the Saints' offense dominated the Lions both in the air and on the ground. Final score: Lions 28, New Orleans, 45.

Detroit fans were pleased with their team despite the loss. The Lions team was proud of its accomplishments. To fans, players, and coaches, *winning = making the playoffs*. Though the Lions didn't take home an NFL Championship title, they still had won.

The Lions were successful for a number of reasons. They had a multidimensional, explosive offense with a number of weapons in their arsenal. They had speed, flexibility, and versatility that freed players up to move the ball. But talent only played a small factor.

More importantly, they had the self-discipline to move the ball. They mentally, physically, and emotionally committed to the game, executed their playbook, and made adjustments when needed to get the next first down. If you want to win your game, you must do the same.

It's not easy for football teams to get first down after first down. Sometimes the team goes three-and-out on a drive. It requires hard work to get the next first down. Achieving your next milestone is no different. Sometimes meeting that marker will come easily. Other times it will be more challenging. Be committed to advancing the ball and make sure you celebrate when you reach it.

Every football team celebrates after they win a game. After every Forest Hills Northern football victory, the players and families would celebrate at the Forest Hills Inn restaurant. It was an opportunity for postgame camaraderie and for everyone to come together as an extended Husky family. We enjoyed the evening while watching high school football highlights. Everyone was fired up for the next game.

While teams celebrate the wins, they're just as excited to get the next first down. The moment is even sweeter if it was a challenge to make it. You must treat each first down as a mini-victory on your life's field. You've worked hard and are getting closer to the end zone, so be sure to recognize this. And when you score, treat yourself to something special. It will fuel you to play harder for the next game.

Playing life's game is tough. Winners know the importance of self-discipline. They knuckle down to get to the next milestone. Even if faced with the blitz or the blindside, great players never lose sight of the next first-down marker. While it may take a while to reach your next checkpoint, unlike football, you don't have four downs to get it. You have built the playbook and can use as many moves as needed to reach the next step. Keep your eyes on the ball, and move it forward.

Coach's Chalkboard

1. Develop milestones to track your progress toward your goals.

2. Execute the playbook to achieve the next checkpoint.

3. Play life's game with a day-to-day commitment to hit the milestone marker.

4. Stay disciplined and remain focused on forward ball movement.

5. Celebrate when you reach the next first down.

"I don't want ordinary people. I want people who are willing to sacrifice and do without a lot of those things ordinary students get to do. That's what it takes to win."

— Bear Bryant

Chapter 10:
Recognize The Blitz

"Football is not a contact sport—it is a collision sport. Dancing is a contact sport. "—Duffy Daugherty

The blitz can hit you from a number of angles. Similar to Baskin Robbins' thirty-one flavors, the blitz playbook offers variety. The *inside zone blitz* is a favorite for many because it contains an extra punch against an inside play. These blitzes usually force the quarterback out of the pocket when he's looking to pass. If this blitz hits the spot, it will stop the run or force the QB to throw the ball under pressure, while he is on the run. I've watched the Chicago Bears turn the ball over many times when up against this play.

The *single-edge zone blitz* is a popular blitz flavor. Here, the defense is hungry, wanting to force the QB to run to the shorter side of the field, effectively limiting his options. The extra-strength *double-edge zone blitz* is a double scoop of blitz that combines blitzing players from both sides of the field for extra pressure.

Another option in the defensive playbook is the *lineman blitz*. The Tampa Bay Buccaneers effectively used this blitz in the early 2000s. The Bucs used quick defensive ends and strong defensive tackles to execute this play. With their speedy defenders rushing off the line of scrimmage and the tackles preventing the quarterback from stepping into the pocket, this play worked for the Bucs. Opponents struggled to make forward progress.

These are only a few examples of the blitz. *Safety blitzes* are often used too. No matter what flavor a defensive coordinator chooses to scoop, the objective is the same: *Pressure the quarterback. Stop the offense. Limit forward progress.*

You are the quarterback in your life. The blitz is relevant because you need to recognize these plays on your football field. Your offensive lineman, your receivers, and your backs are the people who will help you win. They are *with you.* The defensive players are your opponents. Defenders are either people or circumstances that may, intentionally or unintentionally, prevent you from achieving your goal.

In football, the blitz is a strategic move teams use to *intentionally* limit the quarterback's options. The defense hungers for a sack. They thirst for a collision. In life, there are people who *intentionally* want you to

> On your life's football field, people will intentionally try to stop you from moving the ball forward. Recognize the blitz.

fail—they're trying to blitz you. They're driven to knock you down. Forcing a turnover energizes them.

At twenty-nine years old, I was offered a job as a senior manager at Boeing. I eagerly accepted the offer. Such a position within a *Fortune* 50 company seemed exciting and was rarely given to someone so young. I yearned for this increased level of responsibility and could not wait to start this new job. Little did I know what I was getting myself into.

I met all of my peers and direct reports on my first day. It didn't go as planned. While everyone was cordial to my face, the whispers commenced when I walked away.

People continually questioned my qualifications and expertise. An aura of skepticism surrounded me. Many were upset that an *outsider* had stepped into this senior leadership role.

My age impeded employee acceptance. My employees were between fifteen and twenty-five years older than me.

"Who the hell is she?" They questioned. "What does she know about our business?"

"What high school did Suzy pick her up from?"

These comments circulated through the building daily. *I need to find myself amongst this sea of uncertainty,* I thought.

Few people supported me from the onset. I knew this, but I was too blind to recognize how unscrupulous many of my co-workers really were.

I previously worked in an engineering management position at Boeing. In that role, the team and I had developed and executed our playbook. We'd made adjustments when needed. At the end of the day, we completed our challenging engineering objectives. My teams pushed the edges of the technical envelope to demonstrate never-before-seen-capabilities. Because my teams effectively moved the ball, I developed a reputation as a great leader in the company.

This reputation had opened doors for me, including the senior management position I'd recently accepted. While the role was outside of my comfort zone, I was thrilled to undertake a new challenge.

I wanted to succeed. I was committed to learning the business and leading this team effectively. But no matter how hard I worked, I failed to recognize two critical elements. These mistakes meant the blitz would knock me down.

Mistake #1: Don't assume anyone will care that you were great or that anyone will immediately like you.

I was young. I assumed my prior successes had proved my ability to lead. I thought people would immediately recognize why I had earned this job. I was intelligent, respected people and put in the hours. I was sure that once people knew me better, my charismatic personality would win them over.

Not so much.

No one cared about my prior accomplishments. My executive mentors and supporters meant nothing. People focused on my age and the fact that I wasn't home-grown. Nothing I did pleased them; it was never good enough.

Mistake #2: Don't assume people are moral.

I gained supporters over time. I learned the business. But my peers warned me, and I struggled with knowing who to trust. Negative comments continued daily, made by certain cantankerous men—one in particular.

We teach our kids that *sticks and stones can break our bones, but names can never hurt us.* The truth is: *Words often hurt.* My feelings got hurt.

This organization was like no other. Almost every play seemed like a blitz on me. People desired my demise. The possibility of my failure fueled their existence. They did not think such a young person should be in a senior leadership position.

Lesson #1: *Keep your eyes open, work hard to earn people's respect, but don't ever assume that they will be on your team. Figure out who is with you and who is not. Drop the dead weight.*

Others weren't quite as evil. They were merely spectators waiting to see what play came next and how I would react. My offensive line wasn't really my offense. Many were *not with me.* People I trusted turned out to be another defensive tackle, waiting to bring me down.

I was not prepared for the betrayal yet to come. Here came *the mother blitz.*

My boss, Suzy, had hired me into a what-was-supposed-to-be-exciting job. Suzy's unusual leadership style caused most to dislike her. She talked down to people and did not treat all of her employees equally. She often did not practice what she preached. This lack of leading-by-example was a real turn-off for many. Since Suzy promoted me, I thought the relationship between us would be calm and respectable. I was wrong.

Things began well. She mothered me and imparted her astuteness. That quickly changed, and I managed to get on the *bad-list.* I don't know how this happened, but my lack of employee acceptance surely played a part.

Fast forward seven months. I was called into my boss' office. Suzy often summoned her employees on short notice and never told us why. I thought nothing of it. *This was just another day.* Or so I thought.

Little did I know this was my Doomsday.

I was startled to see the Human Resources representative sitting in Suzy's office. *Mindy's here, this can't be good.*

HR and the boss in the room together was an omen.

An ethics complaint had been filed against me. It claimed that I had engaged in conduct that violated our company's business gratuities policy. While the investigation didn't find any violation *per se*, the report stated there was a perception of an impropriety. A disciplinary action was in order.

My sentence: *one-week suspension without pay.*

I held back the tears and hurriedly walked to my office, hoping no one would see me. Shock and disbelief consumed me. *What just happened?*

My employment record with Boeing had been stellar until this point. I didn't think I had done anything wrong. But whether I had violated the policy was not the issue. An investigation had been conducted concluding that an appearance of inappropriate conduct existed. I respected the outcome and took responsibility for my actions.

People make mistakes, and I learned from this one—but the story isn't over yet. What makes this truly heart-wrenching is who filed the ethics complaint: It was my boss. She could have prevented the situation from occurring, but she'd chosen to run a different play. She blitzed me.

In short, I had planned a two hundred-person, week-long conference at my customer's request. The customer had dictated the venue and all meeting arrangements. My company had never paid any money for this event.

As the conference organizer, I needed to arrive early in the morning and leave late each night. For convenience, I decided to reserve a room at the hotel. I called the hotel sales director, who offered to provide a complimentary room.

I hung up the phone and shared the details with my team. Since Boeing did not pay to use the hotel for the conference, I thought this courtesy room would not be considered an inappropriate gratuity. Though I didn't see a problem with this arrangement, others felt differently.

Some people were concerned that my upcoming actions violated Boeing's policies. But no one said a single word to me. However, someone did tell my boss about my plans.

Did Suzy ask me about it? No.

The conference came, I stayed in the hotel, free of charge, and life went on.

Two months later, I was called in for the ethics complaint which resulted in my week-long suspension. I'm not making excuses for what I did. I take responsibility for my actions and accept the punishment. But what makes this story unconscionable is my boss' knowledge of my plans before the event, and her conscious decision to take no action. She'd never approached me about any concerns.

As my director and my manager, Suzy had a moral and an ethical duty to look out for my best interests and the interests of the corporation. She should not have allowed me to engage in actions that could violate company policy. Instead of following the ethical path, she'd waited until I had completed the hotel stay, and *then* had filed an ethics complaint against me.

This act of betrayal and breach of trust left deep wounds. The experience also taught me to recognize the blitz.

Lesson #2: *Be careful who you trust, keep your eyes open, and recognize the blitz.*

In football, the QB and the offense can read blitz and make adjustments. While a blitz can be a very effective way of stopping the ball, it does have its disadvantages. These plays can be very risky for the defense. By running a blitz, the defense is taking away coverage defenders to rush the QB, which usually means the secondary cannot afford to miss any coverage assignments. The defense cannot cover all of the offensive players and is focused on a high-speed force to pressure the quarterback. While they want to sack him, they're also looking to throw off his timing and force poor decision making that could result in a fumble or an interception.

In 2010, the San Francisco 49ers were a team with a losing record. In 2011, San Francisco hired Jim Harbaugh as the new head coach. During this first season, Harbaugh led the team to a 13–1 record and an NFC West Championship. His formula for success: *simplify the playbook.*

Alex Smith was not considered an elite quarterback. But Jim Harbaugh successfully changed Smith's and the offense's approach to the blitz, resulting in a dramatic improvement. Smith now calls proper audibles, converts third downs, and avoids costly mistakes. Due to Harbaugh's simplified playbook, the team is focused on recognizing and beating the blitz.

If you can recognize the blitz, you can make decisions to beat it too. You must use the open players on your team to help you move the ball. This applies in any setting, personal or career.

In my career example, I started at my own two-yard line. My goal was to do a great job in this role and get into the end zone. I didn't care how hard I needed to work or how many hours were required. I was going to cross that goal line and score. Success in this job required making sure my customers were satisfied with my teams' products and services. I knew the goal. The next step was defining the strategy to achieve this.

I had three young children during this time and I needed to balance my role as a parent with my desires to succeed in my new position. My parents were in my support network and I was fortunate to

---

Alex Smith performance with a simplified play-book*:

✓ Improved quarterback rating

✓ Higher completion percentage, average yards per attempt, and TD-INT ratio against blitzes

* Source: *Pro Football Focus*

lean on them for child care if I needed to stay late in the office. I also brought my work home with me and worked on projects and tasks after the kids went to bed. It was important for me to maintain a work-life balance and I made sure to attend my kids' sporting events or other extra-curricular commitments when I was not travelling. I faced a long road ahead if I wanted to get into the red zone, but I wasn't willing to compromise my family's needs to do so. I made sure that I had a support network in place for those occasional times that I could not be available. My family was ready to help me win.

Next, I finalized my playbook. I surrounded myself with people at work who were *with me*. I built my offense and was focused on driving the ball forward.

Offensive linemen can recognize a blitzing player before the snap of the ball. They can communicate with the other players to shift protection to the blitzing player's side, thereby strengthening quarterback protection. The quarterback can also call audibles to signal a protection scheme if coverage seems weak.

In your life, keep your eyes open. Make sure you have coverage when blitzers are trying to take you down. Use your offensive line to be on the lookout for you.

During the following months, I pulled together a strong team: a great offensive line, talented backs, and clever wide receivers who were on board to help me win this game. This cadre of players was ready to march down the field, making necessary adjustments so that we could put some points on the board. I was confident we would cross the goal line.

I had my go-to guys who could make spectacular plays. There were others I could count on for short runs, too. My offensive line was ready to provide needed protection. Those in my inner circle would help me reach greatness.

Playing football and life require more than monumental gains on a single play. When trying to move the ball against the blitz, you can consider running the West Coast Offense. It's an offense that focuses on ball control and short passes. This is a well-timed offense where the quarterback quickly throws the ball to avoid the rush, but after enough time has gone by so that the wide receiver is behind the blitzing players and able to gain some yardage.

> Winning in life requires a combination of short-gains and spectacular plays. Use all players on your offense to move the ball and get the first down.

Be sure to build strategies into your playbook that provide for small and large movements down the field. Don't only focus on teammates who can make spectacular plays. Use the plays that work; eliminate the ones that don't. Short passes and running the ball yourself are also effective moves against the blitz. Great quarterbacks aren't afraid to run the ball themselves if needed. Also, shorter plays can take longer to get to the next first down, but that is ok. What is important is you are still moving the ball downfield.

If you don't read blitz or your offensive line doesn't provide protection, you'll get knocked down. But it's not *game over.*

Do not let those assholes keep you on the ground. If you stay down, they win. Playing on your football field will be a collision sport. If you get hit, get your ass back up.

Let's continue to view the film of my game. There were other

> *"It's not whether you get knocked down; it's whether you get up."*
> —Vince Lombardi

81

people besides my boss who had tried to knock me down. Sometimes they had succeeded. Once I almost didn't get back up.

After enduring months of spiteful comments, backstabbing, and blitzing, I looked for another job within the company. I received an offer to work in the Washington D.C. office in an engineering management role. The job provided more pay, relocation assistance, and a signing bonus. I was ready to close the deal. It was time to move on, and I was not going to look back.

I ran to my peer's office when I received the e-mail offer. He shook his head.

I didn't understand. *This was my ticket out of here.*

"You're leaving for the wrong reasons. You're running away," Chris replied.

I didn't care what the reason was. I was ready for a new job.

I wanted the DC job, but I didn't take it for a number of reasons. Mainly, completing my Juris Doctor was a priority, and I would lose twenty credit hours if I moved to the East Coast.

Chris was right. I was avoiding the problem. I was letting my opponents win. They wanted me to find a new job. They craved for my failure. They were going to run any possible play to force me off the field. Jennifer A. Garrett was a fighter. I was ready to beat the blitz.

When I left that job, I hadn't failed. Those people didn't succeed in keeping me down. Since I was now completely aware of the negative talk around the office, I had my eyes wide open. I was no longer surprised by the amount of effort taking place to try to sabotage my efforts. Sometimes I'm still amazed that people can be like that, but I certainly was not surprised. They wanted to see me fail and were going to try their best to make sure that happened.

But what they didn't succeed at was keeping me down. I'm not going to lie. Playing this game wasn't easy. While being a hard-headed person helped me get through certain collisions, there were days when I would go home, shaking my head, wondering what the heck I had gotten myself into. Yes, there were sometimes nights that I even cried.

But what does not kill us truly does make us stronger. I was determined to move forward on this battlefield. And I did.

When I left that position, I had accomplished much. My customers raved about the products and services my teams provided. I earned their trust and respect. I also received accolades from Boeing executives. I'd won the game.

I would not have been successful without my team. I'd surrounded myself with people that were *with me*. While most of these players did not directly work for me, I had a team of committed people played alongside me on my offense. When opponents blitzed, we knew how to execute. I knew who to throw a pass to, whom to hand the ball off to, and who would provide coverage so that I could get the play off.

The game we play is not an easy one. Not every play you run will work. You *will* get knocked down. You *will* lose yards. It's important that you stay determined and focused. Never stop believing that you'll make forward progress. Take it one play at a time.

Years ago, I watched *The Today Show* interview with then President of Commercial Operations at biotech giant Genentech, Myrtle Potter. She spoke of her accomplishments and mentioned that people told her she wasn't smart enough to achieve such success. In 2002, *Time* magazine included Potter on the *15 Young Global Business Influentials* list.

> *"Never let anyone else determine what your potential is."*
> —Myrtle Potter

The following year, *Fortune* named her as one of the *Top 50 Most Powerful Women in Business.* Potter never let anyone define when she could win. She was in control and determined her potential.

Rule 1: *Never let anyone tell you that you can't do something.*
Rule 2: *Never say that you can't do something.*
Rule 3: *Believe in yourself and think that you can.*
Rule 4: *Play the game of life with your eyes open and be ready to tackle any obstacle.*

Blitzes are advantageous in football because they proactively disrupt the offensive play. They cause pressure on the quarterback hoping to force a turnover, an incomplete pass, or even a sack. If any of these situations occur, the defense has accomplished their objective: The ball does not keep moving down the field. You must read the blitz and react. Do not let them win.

If a blitz is read, your offense can shift protection. Your offensive line can use fundamental blocking principles to stop the blitz and allow you, the quarterback, to get the play off. If your pass is caught, your receiver can navigate through the few remaining defenders downfield. Your team can turn what might have been a minimal gain into a spectacular play. You will have successfully marched down the field.

In my work example, I had offensive lineman who were looking out for me and the team. They would block the defense from trying to sabotage our efforts and I was able to handoff the task (i.e. pass the ball) to one of my teammates who was able to complete the project, making one of our customers very happy.

Remember, the big plays are not the only ones that count. Moving the ball can take time. You may need three or four plays to get the next first down. You must balance the playbook with small and large moves.

Hugh "Duffy" Daugherty was a legendary coach. While he will always be remembered for his impressive routine for winning, he will also be remembered for his big grin, his storytelling, his charm, and his humorous personality.

Daugherty knew football was a collision sport. So is life. From his experiences playing college football and serving in the U.S. Army during World War II, where he earned the Bronze Star, Duffy knew that a person's journey down the fields of life and football will not always be attractive. He trained his players to play a hard game both on and off the field.

> **Coach Duffy Daugherty— Michigan State (1954–1972)**
>
> ✓ Winning career record at MSU (109-69-5)
>
> ✓ Led 1965 and 1966 Spartans to win national championships

In your life, the situation can be a far cry from serenity at times. You will get knocked down at some point, likely more than once. Watch the defenders on your life's field. Your opponents' mission is to sack you. They want to limit forward progress and ensure that you do not move the ball. They eagerly wait for the game clock to expire. Excitement consumes them when the game is over, and you are on the ground.

Take this away from this chapter: *Recognize the blitz. Be aware of the people that are intentionally trying to bring you down, develop your playbook to deal with these opponents, and beat the blitz.*

Coach's Chalkboard

1. Recognize the blitz

2. Develop your playbook to deal with the blitz

3. Adjust to the blitz

4. Beat the blitz

Chapter 11:
Beware Of The Blindside

"There's nothing that cleanses your soul like getting the hell kicked out of you."—Woody Hayes

Y ou *can* recognize the blitz. When you are on your football field, you can spot the defenders intentionally trying to knock you down, and you can beat them. However, blitzers aren't the only challengers in your way. A more powerful force may sack you. You won't know when *the blindside* will hit.

In football, the blindside refers to the side where the quarterback cannot see oncoming defenders. If the quarterback is right handed, his left offensive tackle is expected to provide protection—to cover his blindside. When that coverage breaks down, extra pressure is placed on the quarterback. Often times, he gets sacked.

In life, the blindside refers to unforeseen events that may bring you to your knees. These events hit you like a bullet train before you can even blink. You can't predict when it will happen, but beware that it will. Unlike lightning, it *can* strike the same place twice.

Next to the quarterback, the offensive tackle is the most important offensive position in football. However, you cannot always rely on that coverage to protect you. You *will* get knocked down. Sometimes you *will* lose field position. You must be men-

> Your character is defined by what you do once you have been knocked down.

tally, physically, and emotionally prepared for the blindside. What defines your character is what you choose to do once you have fallen.

Green Bay Packer Aaron Rodgers is an MVP quarterback. He knows his offense and reads the defense better than most. He can read when pressure is coming, whether it's from the blindside, or a blitz, and he protects himself. He quickly evaluates his options and consistently makes big plays in these situations. He is committed to winning, and even if he gets hit by the blindside, he is not going to stay down. While he may be sacked on the first play, he often times capitalizes on the remaining drive and gets in the end zone. Failure is not an option. He gets back up and uses the team, the other players that are *with him*, to make forward progress.

Key to your success is your ability to bounce back once you have been sacked. If you choose to stay on the ground, then it's game over. You have failed. Do

> *"Success is never final, but failure can be."*
> —Bill Parcells

not allow yourself to give up. No matter what unforeseen event has struck you, do not stop playing the game. You may have to delay its completion, but do not lose sight of the goal line.

University of South Carolina running back Marcus Lattimore proved himself as an elite college football player. He was on the rise and destined to go pro. On October 15, 2011 when the Gamecocks played the Mississippi State Bulldogs, Lattimore suffered a devastating injury. He tore a knee ligament, which caused him to miss the remainder of the 2011 season.

Marcus Lattimore was at the top of his game when he collided with this unforeseen injury. The blindside took him down. If he wanted to play football again, he needed to overcome the physi-

Marcus Lattimore Highlights:

Marcus Lattimore Highlights:

✓ 2008 *ESPN RISE* HS Junior of the Year

✓ 2009 *USA Today* High School All-American

✓ 2010 *AP* SEC Freshman of the Year

✓ 2010 *AP* All-SEC 1st Team & 2011 *AP* All-SEC 2nd Team

✓ Set a new school record for 246 rushing yards in a single game (2011 Navy vs. South Carolina)

✓ Set a new school record for 34 career touchdowns (2012)

✓ After his injury, rushed for 120-yards and two touchdowns (2012 South Carolina vs. Kentucky)

cal, mental, and emotional hurdles associated with this type of injury. Lattimore had two choices: *stay down and give up on his dream to play in the NFL, or get back up and keep playing the game.*

Lattimore chose the latter. He recovered and didn't let this setback stop him from moving the ball. In his first game back, he rushed for 110-yards and two touchdowns in a win against Vanderbilt. He then set a school record for career touchdowns in the 2012 game against the University of Alabama at Birmingham. Lattimore was determined not to fail. He was knocked down, but would not remain on the ground.

Similar to an earthquake, the blindside can strike with different magnitudes. A family member may unexpectedly fall sick or get injured. A tumultuous relationship may finally have ended. A catastrophic event may occur such as the death of a loved one, a house burning down, or the loss of a job. You cannot control when these events occur, but you can control how you respond. You must remain focused and determined to rebound. Similar to when a blitzing player knocks you down, do not let this opponent keep you from playing life's game.

When Lou Holtz was the University of Arkansas head football coach, he had the second-best win-loss record in the history of the Southwest Conference. After a 6–5 season, he was fired unexpectedly. Holtz dreamt of coaching at Notre Dame. After losing the coaching gig at Arkansas, he coached for the University of Minnesota, but he never lost sight of his end goal. Two years later, he took over as head coach for a struggling Notre Dame football program. During his eleven seasons with the Fighting Irish, Holtz coached 132 games with an overall record of 100–30–2. Holtz holds the record for most games coached and is second in total victories to Knute Rockne.

Lou Holtz could not control getting fired by Arkansas, but he controlled his ball position on the field. Focused on winning, Lou got into the end zone and won.

Due to the downturn in the economy, a friend of mine unexpectedly lost his job. While it was unfortunate to be suddenly unemployed, Paul was determined not to let this bring him down. In the back of his mind, he had thought about starting his own business but never had the courage to pursue it. Now was his opportunity. Paul formed his new company and is very successful. Similar to Lou Holtz, the blindside had struck Paul. In both situations, they did not let the unexpected event keep them on the ground. You must do the same. Remain in control of your ball movement.

The blindside will hit when you least expect it. The severity of its force will differ every time it strikes. Getting back up can be challenging. The time you need to rebound will vary. No matter how long it takes, you must keep your head in the game. You must have the courage and strength to overcome any event that brings you to your knees. *Winners always get back up.* Reassess your playbook, make necessary adjustments, and move the ball forward.

Coach's Chalkboard

- Beware of the blindside. It will hit when you least expect it to.

- You cannot control when it will knock you down, but you can control how you respond.

- When the blindside takes you to the ground, have the courage to rise again.

- Winners always get back up.

"The real glory is being knocked to your knees and then coming back. That's real glory. That's the essence of it."

—Vince Lombardi

Chapter 12:

Think Before You Punt

"When in doubt, punt."—John Heisman

Football is a game of risk. So is life. When faced with fourth-down decisions, most people take the conservative route. They punt. But great coaches and players think twice before giving the ball to their opponents. First, they weigh all their options. If the situation looks favorable, they go for it. If the risks are too great or they are in doubt, then they punt.

A number of factors are at play. Fourth-and-inches can drive one decision, while fourth-and-long can command a different one. The game clock and field position are taken into consideration as well. The players' mindset determines the next move.

When taking risks, you must believe in yourself and your team. Have faith the outcome will be successful. Philadelphia Eagles head coach Andy Reid was known for taking risks. He believed in his team's ability and, during the 2012 season, went for it twice on fourth down on their own side of the field. The Eagles were successful both times. Decisions like this are not uncommon for Reid. He consistently assesses the situation and trusts the team to make it happen.

Not every risk is worth taking. You must take smart ones. Look at where you are on your field. Where is your next first-down marker? If getting there seems achievable, then go for it.

The first job I took at Boeing was a program manager for the US Army's Future Combat Systems (FCS) program. I was responsible for the successful execution of the FCS program in a US Air Force–sponsored experiment. This was a risky program with a lot of unknowns. I had a team of players committed to meeting all of our objectives. We had a playbook and everyone was willing to work hard to make this exercise a success.

We worked countless hours in the frigid desert to get the systems working. Some days went smoothly. Other days did not. Game time was getting closer, and we were focused on getting into the end zone.

But we didn't just want to score—we wanted to score big. That meant taking more risks than originally planned. In addition to the agreed-upon objectives, the team wanted to push the edges of the engineering envelope. On game day, we wanted to show Air Force and Army generals, members of Congress, and other senior government officials that our program had achieved greatness.

We were clever about the risks that we took. We assessed our situation. We evaluated the tradeoffs associated with taking on other objectives. If we felt it would significantly jeopardize one of our original goals, we punted. If the additional work seemed doable, we went for it. In the end, we exceeded all of our initial objectives and proved much more. All stakeholders and customers were elated. My team had gone for it and won. Our success was later recognized and rewarded by senior Boeing leadership. I became known as a leader who could take risks and execute. This victory led to other exciting opportunities within the company.

In football, teams must have the courage to take risks. It's even more critical in the postseason. When it's playoff time, it's win or go home. There is no tomorrow.

During the 1957 Western Conference game, the Detroit Lions proved their bravery. In the third quarter, San Francisco was leading Detroit 27–7. A 49ers win seemed impending. But the Lions weren't afraid to take risks. Quarterback Tobin Rote rallied the team back with twenty-four unanswered points to win 31–27. The Lions then went on to beat the Cleveland Browns for an NFL championship title. With greater risks come greater rewards.

However, the postseason is not the only time to take risks. The Forest Hills Northern Huskies did just that during the second week of the 2012 season. The Huskies struck early in the game and were leading 14–0. But things turned sour. The defense broke down, and the Byron Center Bulldogs scored twenty-one unanswered points.

With 7:26 remaining, Northern was trailing by seven. They had brutally lost the previous week. The Huskies couldn't bear a second loss so early in the season.

Northern now possessed the ball and controlled their destiny. They picked up four first downs, and then scored a touchdown. The team was within one point of tying. The extra point would get them there.

It was decision time. There was a tomorrow. It was not season over. The next play seemed obvious. Tie the game and hope to win in overtime.

But Coach Rap had a different plan. He believed in his team and decided to go for the win. The Huskies didn't disappoint and scored the two-point conversion. Final score: Byron Center 21, Forest Hills Northern 22.

After the game, Coach Rap publicly praised the team. "It would have been easy [for the

> "A man can be as great as he wants to be. If you believe in yourself and have the courage, the determination, the dedication, the competitive drive and if you are willing to sacrifice the little things in life and pay the price for the things that are worthwhile, it can be done."
> —Vince Lombardi

boys] to pack it in when we went down 21–14. I'm very proud of the way they came back fighting."

What a sweet victory. After this emotional game, Byron Center players boarded their school bus. Some of the players were in tears. They thought a victory was imminent. But they learned the hard lesson that the game was not over until the game clock expired. If you want to win, you must have the courage to take game-winning risks. That is what makes football so exciting. Teams must take chances and play the full sixty. Your life is no different. Step out of your comfort zone, play in the gray zone, and keep driving down the field. It's a must if you want to win.

Remember, playing life's game won't always work out in your favor. But you must try. If you make a decision that does not turn out as planned, then learn from the situation. The only time a risk wasn't worth taking is if you didn't learn from the experience. Reflect on the situation, learn from it, and use that knowledge to move the ball forward.

Furthermore, build contingencies into your plan. If you start down a path that doesn't appear promising, then stop. Assess your field position and determine whether or not you should proceed. Make necessary adjustments. Revisit your playbook. Use your alternate strategies if needed. Can you continue down the path you are on? Or should you execute a different set of plays?

A friend of mine recently told me she was unhappy in her career. It was a high-stress position that didn't afford the flexibility she needed. She wanted to take a lower-paying job that would allow her to pursue personal projects. Her husband was supportive of this change. But they had children who had health issues. She was uncertain of how unforeseen medical circumstances could be covered if she switched professions.

My advice to her was this: *You only live once, so make it count.* It's important to be happy and not live your life with regrets. While it's important to plan for the unexpected, you can't live your life waiting for when the blindside will hit. In her situation, she was concerned with finances. I told her to look at other ways to

> *"He who is not courageous enough to take risks will accomplish nothing in life."*
> —Muhammad Ali

alter the family's lifestyle to survive with the lower income and still be able to put away some money for a rainy day. Then if the blindside hit, and medical bills needed to be paid, they'd have money saved to cover it.

I also told her to believe in herself. She was a strong person, and if she was knocked down, she would figure a way to make life work. *Do not live your life unhappily waiting for something to hit that may never come.* Be prepared, be brave, have a playbook to account for the unexpected, but don't play life's game conservatively. If the situation is so dire that you cannot make the change, then punt. But never lose sight of the end zone. Continually reevaluate, and when the circumstances are right, then go for the score.

Life will continually challenge you. It will put you in situations that test your character and strength. Winners have the drive and the courage to keep going. When the game clock ticks downward, great players press forward. Be a winner. Put your fears aside and go for your dreams. Don't settle; move the ball. Believe in yourself and take the risks needed to win your life's game.

Coach's Chalkboard

- Winners aren't afraid to take risks.

- Assess your situation.

- Have the courage to pursue your dreams.

- If the risks are too great, then punt. Revisit when the time is right. Then go for it, and make it count!

Chapter 13:

Play The Full "60"

"I firmly believe that any man's finest hour, the greatest fulfillment of all that he holds dear, is that moment when he has worked his heart out in a good cause and lies exhausted on the field of battle—victorious"
—Vince Lombardi

The Dallas Cowboys are commonly referred to as *America's team*. According to *Forbes,* the Cowboys are worth more than $2 billion, making them the most valuable US sports franchise.

Throughout the franchise's history, this team proved to fans they knew how to win. The team developed their playbook and executed their plays. Decades of strong coaching and great teamwork fostered the Cowboys' numerous winning seasons.

Former Dallas head coach Tom Landry was committed to winning. During his tenure, he led the Cowboys to twenty consecutive winning seasons, an accomplishment unmatched by any other professional football team. In 1972, Landry and the Cowboys won their first Super Bowl championship together—Super Bowl VI.

"A winner never stops trying."
—Tom Landry

But one Super Bowl victory was not enough. To win this title again, he needed to execute a new play in his playbook. This play involved bringing in an assistant head coach who had the energy and the ambition to achieve greatness. Landry knew exactly who to add to the team. He selected the Cowboys tight end who had scored the final touchdown in the Super Bowl VI win against the Miami Dolphins: Mike Ditka.

During the Landry-Ditka coaching era, the Cowboys proved that they deserved to be *America's team.* The Cowboys were a relentless force known for shutting down their opponents. Any team had better beware of Dallas' Doomsday Defense. During this period, the Cowboys made the playoffs eight times, won six division titles, and three NFC championships. They also won Super Bowl XII in 1978. The Dallas Cowboys of the 1970s were unstoppable.

In 1989, Jerry Jones bought the Dallas Cowboys and fired Tom Landry. He hired Jimmy Johnson as the new head coach. During Johnson's coaching period, the Cowboys dominated the league, winning consecutive Super Bowl titles, making Johnson one of six

> *"Do you want to be safe and good, or do you want to take a chance and be great?"*
> —Jimmy Johnson

coaches in NFL history to achieve such a feat. The Cowboys were relentless, took chances with their playbook, and achieved greatness.

While the Cowboys were a powerhouse during the 1970s and 1990s, the Cowboys of the new millennium failed to live up to expectations. The team frequently disappointed and angered its fans.

Why? The team consistently broke down during games and failed to play the entire game. The Cowboys' biggest shortcoming was mental rather than a lack of talent.

> Coach's Rule: You have to play the entire game if you want to win.

The players were not entirely committed to winning—they didn't have MAD PRIDE.

The team failed to make plays when it mattered most. They lacked mental toughness and didn't play the full sixty minutes of the game.

This principle of playing until the game clock expires holds true in any situation. Executing the playbook throughout the entire game is equally as important in the playoffs, where the rule is *Win or Go Home.*

The Cowboys have been knocked around both in the playoffs and during the regular season. The team has routinely lost fourth-quarter leads and crucial late-season division games. Critical mistakes during the playoffs often knocked the team out of Super Bowl contention.

One game still remembered by NFL fans is the NFC wild card playoff game between the Dallas Cowboys and the Seattle Seahawks on January 6, 2007. The Cowboys were trailing by one point. With 1:19 left in the game, Dallas attempted a nineteen-yard field goal. Quarterback Tony Romo botched the hold by dropping the snap. He tried to run in the end zone for an unplanned touchdown.

Dallas Cowboys

- ✓ Monday Night Football (MNF) against Buffalo Bills, Romo had 5 INT, 1 fumble (2007)

- ✓ Cowboys lost to Philadelphia Eagles 44-6 in a needed late-season division game (2008)

- ✓ Lost 5 season games by giving up 4th-quarter leads (2011)

- ✓ MNF against Chicago Bears, Romo threw 5 interceptions (2012)

Seattle's defensive back Jordan Babineau tackled Romo at the one-yard line. Game over—Dallas was knocked out of the playoffs.

Rule 1: *You must execute the playbook*

Rule 2: *You must make the plays when it matters most*

Rule 3: *You must play the entire game*

One of the greatest Big Ten games occurred on November 22, 1969, at *The Big House*—Ohio State Buckeyes versus University of Michigan Wolverines. Michigan Stadium was packed with 103,588 excited football fans.

Ohio State was the defending national champion. Under Coach Woody Hayes' direction, the Buckeyes were undefeated and the top-ranked team. Michigan's head coach, Bo Schembechler, was redefining the Wolverines' football team—a team some characterized as mediocre.

It was game time. The Buckeyes struck first, scoring a touchdown but missing the extra point. Michigan answered right back with a touchdown and an extra point. Score: Michigan 7, Ohio State 6.

At the end of the first half Michigan was leading 24–12.

The teams traded possessions throughout the second half. With 3:12 left in the game, Woody Hayes called a fake punt. The risky call resulted in a Buckeyes first down. But the Wolverine defense remained strong and quickly squashed the drive.

The Wolverines got the ball, but soon kicked it back to the Buckeyes. Ohio State had one more shot. They fumbled the ball, and Michigan recovered. Game over. Final score: 24–12.

The Wolverines had done it! They had pulled off the greatest upset in college football history. After the game, ABC-TV sports announcer Bill Flemming shouted, "There it is! What has to be the upset of the century."

Similar to the Dallas Cowboys, the Ohio State Buckeyes failed to play the game. They did not execute their playbook. The Buckeyes committed an unheard-of seven turnovers. Michigan, on the other hand, proved they deserved to be the Big Ten champs.

They moved the ball, put points on the board early in the game, and stopped their opponent from scoring. The Wolverines played the entire game and won.

In life, you must keep playing the game until the game is over.

While the principles are the same, the game clock is different. You don't have sixty minutes to score. You control the game time.

PLAYERS MUST ANSWER THE FOLLOWING QUESTIONS:

1. Is my goal still valid?

2. What is my field position?

3. Is my goal achievable in the specified timeframe? If not, can I delay it?

4. How do I adjust to execute the playbook?

COACH'S PLAYBOOK

"What Does it Mean to Win?" described SMART goals—goals that are time-bound. While you set timeframes for your goals, you must continually reevaluate these goals.

Step 1: Is your goal still valid?

"What Does it Mean to Win?" highlighted Brandon Weeden's goal of playing major league baseball. After years playing on minor league rosters, he reassessed his situation. Weeden decided this goal should be crossed off his list. It was time to pursue something different and he refocused on football. Weeden then enrolled in college, played football for the Oklahoma State Cowboys, and became the starting quarterback for the Cleveland Browns in 2012.

Weeden's professional baseball goal was no longer valid. He adjusted and pursued a new goal. Take this away from the first step: *If you don't like the goal or decide it is time to pursue something different, cross it off your list and move on. If your goal is still valid, move on to Step 2.*

Step 2: What is your field position?

You must determine where you are on the football field relative to your goal's deadline. Are you at midfield with one year to go? Are you at midfield with two months to go? Are you at your ten-yard line with three weeks left? Know your field position.

Most parents want to prepare their children to become the best young adults possible when they leave the house after high school graduation. Look at a simplistic example of two families both with sixteen year-old daughters living at home. In Family A, the daughter gets good grades, is involved in school activities, and does not get into any trouble. In Family B, the daughter struggles in school, hangs with the wrong crowd, and often cuts classes.

The goal for Family A and Family B is the same. Both want to raise their daughters to be courteous and responsible individuals in life. However, each family's respective field position is different. From the limited information provided, it appears that Family A is closer to the goal line than Family B. Family A is past mid-field, while Family B is closer to their own twenty-yard line. Assuming Daughter B is passing all of her classes and will graduate on time, both families have two years left on the game clock to meet this goal. Let's follow these families through Step 3.

Step 3: Can you accomplish your goal by your deadline? If not, can you delay it?

Families A and B understand their current field position. By applying Step 2 to your own situation, you too, will know where you are on your life's field. You will also know how much farther you need to drive the ball. Are you close to the end zone? You have your playbook. Now it's time to reexamine your strategy. Is your plan achievable in your specified timeframe? If the answer is yes, commit and focus on getting into the end zone. Execute those plays and move the ball forward. If your deadline is fast approaching, make this goal your first priority. Treat every play as if it were fourth down. Focus on making progress every day and get the first downs. Change your behaviors so you can execute and cross the goal line.

If your goal is unachievable by your stated deadline, what is the impact of delaying it? Circumstances in our lives change. We cannot control everything. It isn't *game over* because you can't achieve your goal within a specified time—extend the game clock.

Currently, Family A and Family B have two years remaining to accomplish their goal. Family A feels like they are on track and there is no need to extend the game clock. Family B is not quite sure. The parents in Family B want their daughter to be a mature and responsible adult before leaving the house at eighteen. Based on their current situation, Daughter B might not be ready to venture out on her own and exhibit the values her parents expect from her.

Family B has a couple of options. They can choose to keep the deadline as is, or they can delay their deadline. They can encourage their daughter to live at home for a few more years while attending college or while working. Regardless of which option Family B chooses, they will need to proceed to Step 4 and identify what adjustments are needed to their playbook in order to accomplish their goal within their defined time horizon.

Step 4: What adjustments do you need to make?

Winning in football and in life both require adjustments. Similar to Family B, you should continually reassess your play-book and make changes when appropriate. Extending your goal's timeframe automatically drives a reexamination of your playbook. How should you adjust your action plan and your strategies for getting in the end zone? You know your field position. You know your gaps. Create your new playbook and execute your plans to fill those gaps. Even if you don't extend your game clock, take a hard look at your current strategy and change it up if needed. Then execute your playbook and don't stop playing the game until you score. You must have a no-excuses mentality. Be relentless.

Chapter 14:
Keep Your Head In The Game

"It's easy to have faith in yourself and have discipline when you're a winner, when you're number one. What you got to have is faith and discipline when you're not a winner."—Vince Lombardi

Playing life's game is tough. There are times when you need to be a fast-mover and a hard-hitter. The same is true in football. Whichever field you are on, one important rule always holds true: *Nothing will go according to plan.* Life will push back on you, just as the defense tries to limit progress on the football field. Regardless of what pours on you, do not stop playing the game. Keep pressing onward.

Success in sports and in life involves hard work, teamwork, discipline, and dedication to the cause. In football, there are many opportunities to win. Week after week, the team gets the chance to beat out another opponent. In life, you have one shot. There is no *I'll play the game later.* You only live once, so make it count. When life throws you back, you must drive forward. Be relentless and never stop moving the ball.

First, you must believe in yourself. Achieving your life's goals starts from within. *Are you with you?* Don't underestimate the power of your mental and emotional being. It's essential to winning. Elite athletes are gifted; that's a given. So are successful business leaders and individuals. They also share another common skill: *the will to win.* Their desire to overcome any obstacle, climb any mountain, and weather through any

> *"Champions aren't made in gyms. Champions are made from something they have deep inside them-a desire, a dream, a vision. They have to have last-minute stamina, they have to be a little faster, they have to have the skill and the will. But the will must be stronger than the skill."*
> —Muhammad Ali

storm is insurmountable. They *want* to win and won't stop until they have crossed the goal line. Similar to great players, you are talented. You must also be committed if you want to win.

Second, you must trust in your team. No one beats life's challenges alone. No football player wins the game without his teammates. Look around you. Do you know *who is with you?* Have you *dropped the dead weight?* Before you continue down the field, ensure there are players in your huddle who will support you. You need winners to help you get into the end zone.

Third, you have identified your goals and developed your playbook. You know you'll need to make adjustments throughout your life. Don't forget one critical play. You need to incorporate the P2P spread into your plan. It's essential to keeping your head in the game.

> *Use the P2P spread to keep your head in the game.*
>
> ➤ Patience to Perseverance

To achieve your dreams, you must have faith, and you must be disciplined. This is simple to say and harder to do. The P2P spread provides the linkage. Having faith in yourself requires patience, while being disciplined involves perseverance. Regardless of the play you are running, keep this in mind:

> *You might not get the first down on your initial attempt. Be patient and keep executing your playbook. When defenders cross over the line of scrimmage, you may get knocked down. Keep your head in the game and have the determination to persevere.*

Martial arts are a lifelong venture. Like every Tae Kwon Do (TKD) student, I started off as a white belt. I progressed through the ranks and am currently a third degree black belt. While time and talent played a role in my TKD achievements, patience topped the list. Earning each black belt required me to perform a series of board-breaking techniques. This is where the patience proved essential.

I was uneasy preparing for my third-degree black belt test. Patterns, sparring, and self-defense moves came naturally for me. But I struggled with the boards. I believed in myself and knew I could overcome this. But practice and hard work was required. On the first few attempts, the boards would not break.

Kick after kick, thrust after thrust, the result was the same. I examined the boards. Not even a crack. I was frustrated and determined not to give up. I could have walked off my field and said the game was over. But that's not how I played. I was a mentally tough girl who stayed focused and ran the P2P spread. I spent countless nights working on my techniques.

My good friend and teammate, Mark, was *with me* on my journey. He coached me at the TKD studio every night, showing me how to adjust my leg movements. Finally it happened! A upsurge of energy consumed my body as my foot penetrated through the boards. I had won. I trained every day afterwards to get ready for my test. The rest is history.

When moving down the field, ask yourself *how bad do I want it?* If your will is strong, you'll accomplish your goals. No matter what obstacles come in your path, you'll persevere.

It was a two and half year journey for me to get commissioned into the JAG Corps. I lived in California when I first applied, but moved to Michigan three weeks before my commissioning date. It was not economically feasible to drill on the West Coast while living out of state. I approached the Michigan Army National Guard and quickly received a new swear-in date.

Remember, life doesn't operate according to plan. I received a phone call two weeks before my ceremony. It was my recruiter. A small, yet painful problem existed. I was not licensed in the state and needed to take the Michigan bar exam. This delayed my commissioning date by at least eight months. I was not happy, but the rules were the rules. I took the bar and passed with ease. Now I was ready again for the JAG Corps. Or so I thought.

I went on a business trip connecting through the Twin Cities. As I walked from one gate to another I listened to my voicemail. My recruiter left me a message informing me that my paper-work had now expired and I needed to start the JAG application process all over. Having gone through this endeavor once, I knew this would be agonizing.

As I sat in the airport, I contemplated this horrible news. *No f'in way...I'm done.* That was my initial impression. I spent an incredible amount of time collecting documents the first time around. Perhaps the JAG Corps was not meant to be. Maybe my game clock had expired. Or had it? In football, the team is limited to sixty minutes of regulation unless overtime extends the game. In life, the game is slightly different. I had some control over when my game was over. I asked myself, *how bad do I want this?* The blind-side had struck and I was determined to win. I wanted to be a JAG officer and I was going to make it happen. I suffered through the process a second time. Six months later I was commissioned into the Michigan Army National Guard JAG Corps. Victory was mine!

The lesson here is if you *want* to beat life's challenges, then you will. When facing the blitz, the blindside, or any other defenders, you must be strong, stay committed and move forward. Sometimes this takes courage, which is another essential element to winning.

In 1970, a plane crash killed thirty-seven players from the Marshall University football team, along with several coaches, trainers, and others. There were no survivors. After this tragedy, the University President considered suspending the football program. But he didn't due to pleas from Marshall students. While the blindside had collided with this community, the Thundering Herd were determined to rise back up. A new coaching staff was hired and a football team was built. The players exhibited courage, made progress, and played the game one day at a time.

Success also involves risk-taking. Getting the next first down sometimes involves uncertainty. Have the courage to try something new. Don't always look to punt. The Marshall community experienced a tragedy wished upon no one, not even our worst enemies. During a time where excuses could have been made, the students were fearless. Their strength was remarkable, and the football program continued on. *They were Marshall.*

The Marshall story is an incredible success story. Sometimes risk taking does not end positively. Hence it is called a risk. In life, there are no guarantees. *Even if you lost today, you must show up tomorrow ready to play.*

That is the slogan for the P2P spread. Be patient. Every day you must strive to advance the ball. The plays won't always work.

> *"You miss 100% of the shots you don't take."*
> —Wayne Gretzky

Opponents will prevent forward ball movement. Learn from the experience. If you never attempt the play, you have no chance of victory. The first step is taking the risk. The second step is growing when you don't succeed.

In football, players review the game film after every game. You must do the same. Reflect back on your actions and use the experience to execute the next play. If you *want* to win, you'll take risks. If the rewards don't materialize, take ownership of what occurred, learn from the situation, and move on. Do not look to blame someone else. It's your life's field. You are the quarterback, you own it, and you control how to respond.

"Play the full '60'" stressed the game was not over until you determined the goal was no longer valid or you passed away. You must keep your head in this game. It can be tempting to give up. Don't do it. Be persistent and continue on. You have found your greatness, now realize it.

Achieving greatness occurs at any age. From young children to the elderly, it's never too late to realize your dreams. If you set your mind to winning, you'll win. A varsity football team from Middletown, Connecticut fully appreciated this and embraced the essence of perseverance in an unprecedented comeback victory.

On October 26, 2012, the Xavier Falcons played the Hillhouse Academics. By the end of the first half, the Academics were leading 28–14. At the close of the third quarter, Hillhouse commanded a twenty-one point lead. The outcome seemed inevitable in Hillhouse's favor. However, on any given game day, any team can win. This is why I loved football as a kid. On game day my eyes were glued to the television because *the game is not over, until the game clock has expired.* Xavier proved this to be true on that chilly Friday night.

In the movie, *Any Given Sunday*, Cameron Diaz played the character of Christina Pagniacci, who said, "No intensity, no victory." During the fourth quarter, the Xavier Falcons played with immense intensity, completely focused on getting the victory. With a three-touchdown spread, tying the game seemed impossible. The Falcons *wanted this win.* They closed the lead to within seven. Then they scored another touchdown. The score was now 48–49. It was decision time. If they kicked an extra point, the game would be tied. If Xavier went for a two-point conversion, they would win the game. Life and football involve taking risks. The Falcons went for two and got it. They won the game 50–49!

> *"You can learn more character on the two-yard line than anywhere else in life."*
> —Paul Dietzel of LSU

Nancy, a colleague of mine at GE, had a son named Max who played for the Xavier football team. I saw her three days after the game and she had an incredible glow about her. As she described the game to me, I could picture myself in the stadium. What an amazing experience for a high school football team. The lessons those players learned from this game are priceless. In life, and in football, *do not give up at halftime. Play the game until it's over. You can make what seems impossible a reality.*

The Xavier Falcons were fired up after that game. They then carried this energy with them through the postseason match-ups. On December 7, 2012, Xavier played their final game of the year at Rentschler Field (UConn Stadium) where they became the 2012 Class LL Connecticut State Champions. Way to go Falcons!

Life is full of challenges. Greatness won't come overnight. My good friend once told me, *without the bad, the good isn't that great.* Think about it. If you were in the red zone where defenders stopped you play after play, you would feel incredible once you crossed the goal line. Compare when you achieved a goal without hurdles to one where you worked tirelessly to overcome the obstacles. In these scenarios, your emotional state falls in a different spot on the positivity continuum. In the former you may be content, while in the latter you likely will be triumphant on steroids. As human beings, we enjoy beating challenging goals more so than easy ones.

If you want to win life's game, your head, heart, and guts must be aligned. You must be committed mentally, physically, and emotionally to playing on the field every day. No excuses. You must take risks and learn from them when you do not succeed. Look in the mirror and ask yourself, *how bad do I want this?* If you want it bad enough, then run the P2P spread while executing your playbook, train like an athlete, have MAD PRIDE, and score. Don't let anyone or anything stop you.

Coach's Chalkboard

- If you want to achieve your goals, you will make it happen.
- You must be patient and have perseverance.
- Every day matters, so make each one count.
- Have the courage to try something new.
- What you think seems impossible, really is possible.
- The game is not over, until you say it's over.

"Don't give up at half time. Concentrate on winning the second half." —Bear Bryant

Chapter 15

Train Like An Athlete—Have MAD PRIDE

"For me, winning isn't something that happens suddenly on the field when the whistle blows and the crowds roar. Winning is something that builds physically and mentally every day that you train and every night that you dream."—Emmitt Smith

What makes a great athlete great? Many elements constitute greatness—and talent alone doesn't get you there. Of course an athlete has to be talented. But achieving greatness encompasses much more.

I've identified fundamental concepts that contribute to the making of a good athlete. But this chapter will discuss eight key factors that separate the good from the great. It's easy to remember, too. To be great, you need to have MAD PRIDE.

MAD PRIDE

Mental Toughness	Practice with Purpose
Ambition with Attitude	Relentlessness to Rebound
Determined Balance	Improvement Focused
	Dedication to a Healthy Diet
	Energy that Energizes

During the Olympic Games, we watch some of the world's best athletes compete. In the summer 2012 Olympics, the US Women's gymnastics team won the gold medal, a feat not achieved since 1996. These athletes perform at this level because of their commitment to training not only physically, but mentally as well.

To train like a great athlete, you must be committed to winning. You must *want it* enough. Your inner spark must be charged and ready to detonate.

> *"It's not the size of the dog in the fight, but the size of the fight in the dog."*
> —Archie Griffin often quoted this Mark Twain saying

At five-foot nine, Archie Griffin was smaller than most football players. But Archie was driven and determined to excel. He had ambition with attitude and showed the world of football that the little guy could be great. Griffin won the Heisman trophy not once, but twice.

Archie Griffin was amazing. You can be like Archie on your life's field. You can achieve greatness. Athletes find the mental, physical, and emotional strength to persevere through adverse situations. You must do the same.

Let's examine the eight components that make up MAD PRIDE.

Chapter 16:
Mental Toughness

Mental Toughness is what gives you the edge over your competition. Toughness is mental, physical and emotional. Dr. David Yukelson, Penn State's Coordinator of Sport Psychology Services at the Morgan Academic Support Center for Student-Athletes, stresses the need for Mental Toughness. He says mental toughness is the "natural or developed psychological edge" that enables individuals to cope better than their opponents when faced with the many demands of life.

Being mentally tough encompasses many qualities.

First and foremost, mental toughness means staying focused, not being adversely affected by your opponents or distracted by your critic within. This focus requires blocking out what's not important. You must ignore any and all distractors and detractors. Block them out. Kick them off of your football field. Leave them on the sidelines. They should not be in the field of play.

Second, mental toughness requires you to condition or recondition your mind to think confidently. You must ensure that you *always* think positive thoughts. You must maintain the confidence that you can overcome any obstacle or recover from any setback.

Third, mental toughness means never giving in. Do not let anyone break you. Stay committed to moving that ball forward. You must beat the blitz, you must overcome the blindside, and you must get into the end zone.

Fourth, mental toughness is about the mental, physical, and emotional conditioning needed to balance the lifestyle of a great athlete. All three of these elements are important if you want to win. You'll learn more about balance in "Determined Balance".

Great athletes do not focus exclusively on the physical aspects of training. Physical talents won't be enough. All good coaches know that the mental side of sports is what separates those with potential from those who achieve. Great athletes know the significance of mental toughness and spend the time needed to develop it. Mental toughness *truly* is the edge that separates elite athletes from the mediocre.

Coach's Chalkboard

Mental toughness requires conditioning your mind, your body, and your emotional self.

"Mental toughness is essential to success."
—Vince Lombardi

Chapter 17:
Ambition With Attitude

Great athletes are obsessed with winning. They have the motivation and the drive to stay focused and continually move the ball forward. It's this winning attitude that gives them an edge and separates them from their competition. In addition to having a yes-I-can attitude, they're ambitiously fired up and use that go-getting energy source to drive them toward their goals.

This is what I call Ambition with Attitude. Great athletes possess an extra spunk that keeps them going. They know what their goals are and are driven to accomplish those goals, no matter what they must overcome.

In "What Does it Mean to Win?" you learned about identifying your goals. You should have written yours goals down. Without writing down your goals, it's easy to convince yourself that you are busy doing other things. Your goals keep getting bumped down your priority list. Sound familiar?

We have all done this. But at the end of the week, the month, or the year, we are unhappy because we didn't pursue our goal. When you feel this way, what do you need to do? Make winning a priority today.

When Vince Lombardi was head coach of the Green Bay Packers, he not only wanted to win, he wanted to win now. Winning today was the only acceptable answer. His players were motivated by the fear of letting Coach Lombardi down. He pushed his players every day both on and off the field. These athletes were fired up about winning. There was no other suitable outcome.

While "Check Your Ego On and Off the Field" focuses on having a humble and positive attitude, "Ambition with Attitude" addresses what needs to be at your core. No matter which of life's games you are playing, you *must* play it with heart.

In 1993, TriStar Pictures released the popular sports movie *Rudy*, based on the life of Daniel "Rudy" Ruettiger, who dreamed of playing football at Notre Dame. Obstacles stood in his way, including financial challenges and dyslexia. But Rudy was determined, and he had heart. He persevered and got accepted to Notre Dame as a transfer student. In 1975, Rudy finally got his chance to play for the football powerhouse. Coach Devine sent in the walk-on football player for the last play of the game. Rudy sacked the Georgia Tech quarterback. Rudy had done it. He realized his dream—Rudy wanted to play Notre Dame football, and he won!

Playing with heart means giving one-hundred percent of yourself all the time. As a kid, I idolized Walter "Sweetness" Payton. His determination to move the ball and make spectacular plays was incredible. During his career, he led the NFL in career rushing with 16,726 yards. Though Emmitt Smith has since broken the record, Walter Payton is recognized as one of the greatest running backs of all time, mostly because he had heart. He had ambition with attitude.

You must have heart when playing on life's football field. When you want to achieve your goals, go in full-force, and don't stop until you have crossed that goal line. Have Ambition with Attitude, and be relentless.

Coach's Chalkboard

Ambition with Attitude requires:

1. A clear understanding of your goals
2. An obsession with winning
3. Playing the game with heart—giving 100% all the time

"I want to be remembered as the guy who gave his all whenever he was on the field."—Walter Payton

Chapter 18:

Determined Balance

My son attended UCLA coaching legend John Wooden's basketball camp during the summers. Coach Craig Impelman, former UCLA assistant coach, ran the week-long sessions. During a warm-up talk, Coach Impelman told the kids, "Balance is one of the most important words in the dictionary."

I could not agree more. We are all busy people. Because of this craziness, we find it hard to balance work, life, and family. Great athletes are no different from us. They have hectic schedules as well. However, these athletes make conscious decisions to live a balanced life. They have Determined Balance. They make time to hang out with the family, to eat right, to rest, to find personal time, and so on.

If you ask my friends what they think of me, you would hear two comments. First, people say I'm nuts for taking on as much as I do. But second, they say "I don't know how she does everything."

In spite of working fifty- to sixty-hour weeks, keeping a crazy travel schedule, and going to gymnastics, football, and cheerleading events, I find time to decompress.

Things can get stressful, and that is why it's important for you and me to have determined balance. Make a balanced lifestyle a *priority*. It not only helps you in the here-and-now, but keeps you healthy for years to come.

I never said achieving determined balance would be easy. You may not be in a financial situation where you feel like you can do that. It's tough working two or three jobs. This is a rough economy, and we make choices that are best for the family. But remember, it's also important to take care of you.

> Determined Balance requires mental, physical, and emotional well-being.

Great athletes take care of themselves on a number of levels—physically, emotionally, and mentally. They have mental toughness and ensure they have a healthy, balanced routine. Build physical activity into your weekly schedule. To find the time, you must commit to making it happen. Whether that means you wake up earlier in the morning to go for a walk, or you hit the gym after work, just do it. You'll feel better, and you'll have more energy to focus on your goals, to focus on *winning*. Determined balance requires prioritizing activities and making choices that lead to that balanced lifestyle.

Maintaining a healthy diet is also an important aspect of determined balance. While I won't tell you what you should or should not eat, there are fundamental principles that can guide you. You'll learn more in "Dedication to a Healthy Diet".

Determined balance involves making good choices, and not only dietary ones. You need sound decision-making in all aspects of your life—physical, mental, and emotional. This includes getting enough rest. How often have you struggled through the day while not-on-your-game because you were tired? It can be tough, but sleep is essential for a healthy you.

Research shows the benefits of adequate sleep. Mark Stibich, Ph.D., published "Top 10 Health Benefits of a Good Night's Sleep" on About.com. Stibich highlights benefits like reduced stress, a healthier heart, weight loss and a smarter you. In order to move that ball, you need to be on your A-game. You need mental toughness and determined balance. Proper sleep will help you achieve both. Make the decision to balance your life with proper rest. Don't forget to incorporate exercise, meditation and a proper diet into your lifestyle.

Smart choices are critical to having determined balance. But there is a difference between going-for-it-on-fourth-down-and-not-converting and dumb choices. As mentioned in "Think before You Punt", it's okay to take risks. In fact, it's encouraged. Even if you fail, you only *really* fail if you didn't learn anything from the situation. Learning is how we get stronger. It helps us get into the red zone. It helps us cross the goal line.

Dumb choices, on the contrary, are decisions you make that could have adverse impacts on your life and potentially the life of others. People often make these decisions when not thinking clearly, or if they don't care. Drinking and driving is a perfect example. I'm sure you can recall a story of a drunken driving fatality.

Determined balances requires an *awareness* of the actions you are about to engage in and the potential impacts. This balance requires understanding the consequences when choices may question your moral compass or violate legal constructs.

Ricky Williams started high school at 5'9" and 155 pounds. As a high school running back, he rushed for a total 4,129 yards and 55 touchdowns. He won the *San Diego Union-Tribune's* 1994 Player of the Year Award during his senior year. Williams went on to play football for the University of Texas. He dominated college football in the late 1990s. Destined for pro-football, Williams held or tied twenty NCAA records during his collegiate career.

Every boy who plays college football dreams of one day playing in the NFL. Ricky Williams was no different. Based upon his impressive college record, the NFL expected much for this up-and-coming professional athlete.

Coach Mike Ditka strongly believed in Williams and traded all the New Orleans Saints 1999 draft picks in order to get him. Confident the marriage would work, Ditka and Williams posed for the cover of *ESPN The Magazine* as a bride and groom with the heading "For Better or For Worse."

Ricky "Texas Tornado" Williams
U. of Texas Highlights:

✓ NCAA Division I-A career rushing leader with 6,279 yards (later surpassed by Ron Dayne from Wisconsin)

✓ 1998 Heisman Trophy Winner

The "for better" never materialized. Williams played a mediocre first three seasons with the Saints. After being traded to the Miami Dolphins, things improved slightly. He led the NFL with 1,853 rushing yards and earned a trip to the Pro Bowl.

But as quickly as Williams' career progressed, it took a turn for the worse. In May 2004, the NFL announced that Williams had tested positive for marijuana use. He failed a second drug test and was rumored to have failed a third. The league suspended Williams for substance abuse violations. Williams clearly lacked regard for his choices and learned nothing from his previous actions.

When Williams officially returned to the Dolphins in July 2005, his performance was less than spectacular: 743 yards, six touchdowns. His career continued to spiral downward.

In February 2006, the NFL announced Williams' fourth drug policy violation, which resulted in a suspension for the entire 2006 season. In May 2007, it was reported that he'd failed a fifth drug test. While Williams was later reinstated to the league, his mediocre performances continued.

Williams, once thought to be destined for greatness, never lived up to expectations. He accomplished a remarkable high school football career and possessed an impressive college football record. While he could have been an NFL great, Williams' decision-making failed the reasonableness test. Williams made dumb choices and lacked determined balance. As a result, Ricky Williams never got past ordinary. He was so close, but yet far from being extraordinary.

Determined balance requires a controlled focus on appropriate actions and a commitment to not overtax your body or your mind. It requires getting enough rest to ensure that you are recharged physically, mentally, and emotionally. Leading a balanced personal life will help you on all levels. Make time just for you. Determined balance will eliminate stress, and you'll be happier. Once you strive for a balanced lifestyle, moving the ball down your football field will be easier. Treat yourself right, and you'll be closer to achieving greatness.

Coach's Chalkboard

- Determined Balance requires making smart choices.
- Build physical activity into your weekly routine.
- Get plenty of rest.
- Make a balanced lifestyle a priority.
- Train like a great athlete and take care of yourself on all levels—mental, physical, and emotional.

Chapter 19:

Practice With Purpose

Never underestimate the importance of practice. In all sports, including the game of life, practice is an essential part of winning.

After two seasons at Georgetown, Allen Iverson was selected first overall by the Philadelphia 76ers in the 1996 National Basketball Association (NBA) draft. At six feet tall, Iverson became the shortest first-overall draft pick ever.

In a sport dominated by big guys, Iverson excelled and demonstrated his talents. He earned the NBA Rookie of the Year award.

Iverson's talents landed him a spot on the NBA All-Rookie First Team. He continued to shine during his early years in the NFL. In 2001 and 2002, Iverson achieved consecutive scoring titles, averaging over thirty points per game both seasons.

The 76ers squeaked into the playoffs in the 2002 season. The Boston Celtics knocked the 76ers out after a 3–2 series. Head coach Larry Brown publicly criticized Iverson for missing team practices. On May 7, 2002, this is a partial of how Iverson responded in a press conference:

Allen "The Answer" Iverson:
NBA Highlights

✓ Rookie season: 23.5 average points per game, 7.5 average assists per game, and 2.1 average steals per game.

✓ 2001 NBA All-Star MVP

✓ 2001 NBA Most Valuable Player (at 6'0" and 165-lbs, Iverson was the shortest and lightest player to win this award)

"I mean listen, we're sitting here talking about practice, not a game, not a game, not a game, but we're talking about practice."

"Not the game that I go out there and die for and play every game like it's my last, but we're talking about practice, man."

"How silly is that?"

Iverson used the word *practice* twenty times during the press conference. With my eyes glued to the television, my jaw dropped in disbelief. How could a talented athlete be so foolish?

Similar to life and football, basketball is a team sport. If a team wants to win, the team must practice together so they can play like a team. No player is a superstar without practice. They must always work on some aspect of their game. There is a purpose to practice.

Iverson is not alone in his misguided views. Many football players discount the need to practice. Recently, Seantrel Henderson, University of Miami offensive tackle and 2009 *USA TODAY* High School Offensive Player of the Year, was criticized for both showing up to practices late and missing entire practices.

Anyone seen Seantrel?

Frank Leahy, former Notre Dame Head coach (1941–1943, 1946–1953) led the Fighting Irish to four national title championships in the 1940s. Coach Leahy believed games were won in practice and was known for being a stickler. Hitting occurred in every

> *"Lads, you're not going to miss practice unless your parents died or you died."*
> —Frank Leahy

practice and he made quarterbacks catch snaps until their hands bled. His relentless coaching style resulted in well-conditioned teams that were physically, mentally, and emotionally tough.

Athletes who do not practice are far from great. Similar to football, achieving your personal and professional goals involves hard work and practice. Great athletes commit to winning, dedicate time for improvement, and practice their game. Great athletes practice with purpose. You must do the same.

In the career setting, even top performers need to practice. "Check Your Ego on and off the Field" focuses on never thinking you are good enough. You must maintain an improvement mindset and practice if you want to win.

Rashaan Salaam Pre-NFL Player Highlights:

✓ All-American high school football star

✓ 1994 Heisman Trophy Winner

✓ At University of Colorado, set season rushing school-record 2,055 yards (only 1 of 4 college RBs to have 2,000-yard rushing in a single season)

Former Chicago Bears running back Rashaan Salaam was bound to be a professional football sensation. After a spectacular junior year at the University of Colorado, Salaam declared himself eligible for the NFL draft. On April 22, 1995, the draft began at Madison Square Garden. Salaam sat backstage in the "green room" of the Paramount Theatre with dozens of other football players, their families, friends, and agents waiting for their name to be called. Many people didn't think it would take long before they heard, "the [team] selects Rashaan Salaam…"

A number of running backs piqued the interest of NFL coaches. Washington's Napolean Kaufman, Michigan's Tyrone Wheatley, Tennessee's James Stewart, and Penn State's Ki-Jana Carter eagerly sat backstage too.

The first-round picks began. The Cincinnati Bengals selected Ki-Jana Carter as the No. 1 draft pick. Wheatley, Kaufman, and Stewart were called in the first twenty. Surprised Salaam was still available, Head coach Dave Wannstedt picked Salaam as the No. 21 first-round pick. Bears fans celebrated the selection.

At 6'1" and 210 pounds, Salaam was strong enough to take NFL-level punishment. He possessed the quickness and clever moves to make spectacular plays and score touchdowns. Salaam quickly made his mark on the Bears. Many Sunday mornings, my neighbors could hear me yelling at the television: "Run, Salaam run."

Salaam set an impressive Bears rookie record—1,074-yards rushing and ten touchdowns.

The new kid appeared to be a rising star. But this soon changed. While Salaam's nine fumbles were overlooked, injuries and heavy marijuana use caused his demise. Similar to Ricky Williams, Salaam ended up another football has-been that could have been great.

In a 2012 interview with *Chicago Tribune's* Fred Mitchell, Salaam talked about his former NFL career. "Work on your game. I didn't realize coming up how much work you had to put in once you got to the NFL," he said. "It's a whole different lifestyle. You have to change the way you live. You have to change who you hang out with. You have to totally get focused on your game. You have the athletic ability, but if you don't put the work behind it, nothing will come from it."

If you want to move the ball on your football field, you must commit to winning. You must practice with purpose and put in the hard work. You must make lifestyle changes—remain focused, maintain a visual on the first-down marker, and execute the playbook.

The chances of playing professional football are slim. According to the National Federation of State High School Associations, one million high school students participate in football annually. Only one in seventeen will play college football. The National Collegiate Athletic Association (NCAA) stated that only one in fifty college seniors are drafted by an NFL team. This translates into .09% of high school senior football players getting drafted into the NFL.

As a college running back, Rashaan Salaam demonstrated his talents. He wanted to play in the NFL. He got that chance. But making it onto the roster was just the first step. To be a great professional athlete, he needed practice with purpose.

Your personal goals are no different. Practice is essential to move the ball downfield.

If your goal is to play a musical instrument, countless hours of practice are required to master that skill. I started playing piano when I was four years old. My parents saw my potential as a pianist and made me practice for hours each day. Though my friends got to play outside, I sat on the piano bench.

As a kid, I didn't always want to practice. My mom forced the discipline. Though I oftentimes wanted to be with my friends, practice taught me an invaluable lesson. *You must commit to practicing if you want to win.* I never would have mastered Beethoven's *Moonlight Sonata* without practice.

I started training in Tae Kwon Do when I was twenty-two. In order to progress to the next belt level, certain milestones and requirements must be met. Many beginning martial artists want to become a black belt. I was no different.

I wanted the honor of wearing a black belt one day too. That was the goal, i.e. what it meant to win. To practice with purpose, I needed to:

1. *Commit to winning*
2. *Practice the skills needed for the next belt level*
3. *Make no excuses*
4. *Practice with 100% effort all the time*

Determined to achieve this goal, I attended class four days a week. I practiced at home daily as well. In my home practice sessions, I focused on mastering the skills needed to meet the black belt requirements. I earned my black belt in two and a half years. I continued to train, purposely practicing to become a higher level martial artist. Today, I am a third-degree black belt.

In order to be great, you need to work at it. In order to win, you need your teammates. Every time I tested for a black belt, my support network trained with me, pushed me, and would not quit on me. At times I was frustrated because I could not master a technique. My teammates drove me to work harder and to win. Do not underestimate the power of your team. Use your team to stay focused, execute your playbook, move the ball downfield, and score the touchdown.

Some plays will be easier to execute than others. Recognize that life will continually throw challenges at you. Work hard towards achieving your goals—for without the bad, the good isn't really that great. Feel the bitter sweetness when you cross over that goal line.

In the career setting, we often want a promotion. But are you ready for the promotion? Have you mastered the skills you need? Are you financially savvy? Do you know enough about the business? Ask yourself the following questions:

1. *What do I need to know to position me for my next job?*
2. *How can I use my current job to acquire these skills?*

One of my mentors told me, "Always make your job a little bigger than what it's supposed to be." This involves additional work. If you want to rise onto a higher playing field, you must work harder. Most people do not want to do more work. Separate yourself from the ordinary, and be extraordinary. Once you have done this, you'll be practicing with purpose.

Salaam discussed his failure to make a lifestyle change once in the NFL. This is an important component to winning. "Are You With Me?" focused on two things: surrounding yourself with supporters, and eliminating the distractions and detractors.

You need your teammates to win. You must also drop the dead weight.

Attending law school was a huge sacrifice for my family and me. I worked fulltime and attended evening classes while raising three children as a single parent. It was difficult. Some days, I slept in the school parking lot before class. Occasionally, I slept through the first hour of class. While that was not ideal, it was reality. *You find a way by altering your lifestyle in order to achieve your goals.*

To complete law school, I made sacrifices. I prioritized my life and developed my playbook. I scaled back my Tae Kwon Do training. My social life was nonexistent. I had the discipline to focus on my law school playbook, and these other activities were put on hold.

In the same *Chicago Tribune* article, Salaam recalled, "I had no discipline. I had all the talent in the world… The better you get, the harder you have to work. The better I got, the lazier I got."

Similar to Ricky Williams, Rashaan Salaam could have been an NFL great. Both had accomplished much at the collegiate level, but because of the choices they made, they ended up mediocre. Great athletes recognize the need for practice. They have discipline and practice with purpose. You must do the same.

Coach's Chalkboard

Practice with Purpose involves:

- Commitment to the goal

- Discipline to execute the playbook

- Making the lifestyle change to implement the playbook

- Surrounding yourself with supporters and dropping the dead weight

- A no-excuses mentality

"Nobody who ever gave his best regretted it."

—George S. Halas

Chapter 20:
Relentlessness To Rebound

Relentlessness means never losing sight of the ball on life's football field. It means staying committed to moving the ball forward, to getting into that end zone, and to scoring. No matter what obstacles you face, you must have Relentlessness to Rebound.

Dorial Green was used to adversity. His mother had substance-abuse problems, and he never knew his biological father. Green faced emotional instability and uncertainty as a foster kid who bounced from home to home. None of these obstacles kept Green down. He became a shining star. His high school coach, John Beckham, recognized Green's amazing character and adopted him in 2009, which is when he changed his name to Dorial Green-Beckham.

In high school, Green-Beckham dominated against other wide receivers and was named All-time national career receiving yards leader. "I'm real excited to have this record stand in my name for however many years," Green-Beckham told ESPN. "This is the top moment for me."

During Green-Beckham's high school football career, he posted an impressive 6,447 receiving yards, which included a 354-yard game. He continued to amaze at the University of Missouri and was named the 2011 *USA TODAY* Offensive Player of the Year.

No matter what challenges Green-Beckham had faced in his adolescent years, he was determined to not let that adversity play a factor in football. He showcases what every great athlete needs to possess—the relentlessness to rebound.

"The Pre-Game Show" highlighted how the John Tyler Lions almost lost an important football game to the relentless Plano East Panthers. The Panthers came back from a huge deficit and proved the win wasn't locked up until the game clock expired. While the Lions bounced back to pulled off the victory, they almost lost. Due to their relentlessness, the Lions were able to rebound. They won.

There truly is nothing like getting the hell knocked out of you, either literally or figuratively. These events cause us to evaluate what we stand for and what are values are. They force us to make a choice: *give up or keep going.*

In "Recognize the Blitz," you read how I got the hell knocked out of me. Emotionally shaken and uncertain of the future, I got back up. I had fallen. But now it was time for revenge of the fallen. I mentally committed to moving that ball forward and was determined to win. No matter what those blitzers tried to do, they weren't going to stop me.

Whenever I faced an obstacle, I used *mental toughness* coupled with *ambition with attitude* to be relentless. I was determined to learn from any setback and used that knowledge to make me stronger—mentally, physically, and emotionally.

You cannot always control what happens to you. You might not see the blitz. You will be victim to the blindside. But you can control how you respond. No matter who or what challenges you, remember this: Rise above these obstacles and have the relentlessness to rebound.

Coach's Chalkboard

1. Never lose sight of the end zone.

2. You can't always control what happens to you, but you can control how you respond.

3. Rebound and move the ball forward.

4. Use Mental Toughness and Ambition with Attitude to be relentless.

Chapter 21:

Improvement Focused

Great athletes focus on continuous improvement. This improvement focus is essential to winning on the football field and in life. An improvement mentality requires running the *Triple Option.*

TRIPLE OPTION:

---

1) Identify where the improvement is needed

2) Invent the playbook

3) Implement the playbook

COACH'S
PLAYBOOK

While "Check your Ego both On and Off the Field" addressed continuous improvement, the *Triple Option* complements that principle. This option requires dedicated focus to self-improvement. You start with a mindset that incorporates continuous improvement into your regimen. These principles apply to both personal and career goals.

In football, conditioning plays a critical component in playing the game. While playing high school football, my son Anfernee realized he needed to make improvements to his performance. Though he was not overweight, he needed to shed a few pounds of body fat. Additionally, he needed to build up his physical strength.

Anfernee developed his playbook. He changed his lifestyle. He lifted weights every day after school, both during the football season and in the off-season. He improved his diet. The football program showed him the value of conditioning. The effects not only helped his athleticism, but improved his health and led to a balanced routine. His improvement mentality drove him to move the ball.

If you are looking to bulk-up or just lose some weight, the same improvement mentality applies:

Rule 1: *Identify where the improvement is needed*
Rule 2: *Invent the playbook*
Rule 3: *Implement the playbook*

Consult your physician before engaging in a new exercise routine or making significant modifications to your current workout. Include a healthy diet as part of your playbook, too.

The Triple Option helps focus you on moving the ball forward. It's a play you can apply to any situation.

Years ago, I wanted to buy a new car. I didn't need a new car, but I *wanted* a new car—an Acura TL. For practical reasons, I had foregone buying a sports car. Driving a sports utility vehicle has its family benefits, but a sports car is more exciting for us car buffs. One day, I would achieve my goal of owning a sports car. I would find a way to make it happen.

The time came four years later. Before I purchased my dream car, I ran the Triple Option.

Step 1: Identify what you need to improve—*my budget situation.*

While I could absorb the car payment without making significant changes to my finances, this would leave little money remaining for a rainy day. I didn't like that. Improvements and changes to my spending needed to be made.

Step 2: Invent the playbook—*Look for areas I could cut unnecessary expenses.*

This required examining all outgoing expenses. Since I used a financial planning spreadsheet to track my monthly expenses, it was easy to identify how much money was going where. I put a critical eye on every category and questioned those expenditures. Did I need to spend so much money eating out? Was it necessary to buy so many beauty products? Could I cut out some clothing spending?

After examining each area, I developed my playbook with budget adjustments. Step 2 complete.

Step 3: Implement the playbook—*Stick to my new budget allocations.*

If I wanted this car, I needed to execute my plan. In "Determined Balance" and "Practice with Purpose," lifestyle changes were examined. My plan included a new budget. Lifestyle changes would happen as a result. In the end, I reduced my discretionary spending and bought my Acura TL—a Type S even!

The Triple option worked for me. I identified where I needed to improve, developed my playbook, and executed the plays. My playbook involved sacrifice and change. I love my car and have no regrets. I won that game. Look at your goals and make the Triple Option work for you. Be creative and willing to push yourself into the *gray zone.* Your strategy should stretch beyond your comfort level. Then you have to execute your plan. Be Improvement Focused.

Coach's Chalkboard

Improvement focus requires a commitment to self-improvement. The Triple Option works for any situation:

- ✓ Identify what improvement is needed
- ✓ Invent the playbook
  - Think creatively on what the playbook needs to be
  - Stretch beyond your comfort zone
- ✓ Implement the playbook
  - The ones who win games are the ones who can execute their plays

Chapter 22:
Dedication To A Healthy Diet

No matter what your goals are, exercise, sleep, and Dedication to a Healthy Diet are essential. Great athletes know this and stay committed to achieving determined balance.

You need determined balance to accomplish your goals. Part of this balance requires maintaining a healthy diet. Exercise and a proper diet are two of the most pivotal elements in determining your health and well-being. Helpguide.org is a useful resource where you can find a plethora of articles dedicated to diet, as well as exercise. The President's Council on Fitness, Sports & Nutrition (www.fitness. gov) also provides valuable information for a healthy diet and balanced lifestyle.

> *"Eating properly is great. I mean you cut the fat down, cut the cholesterol out, but still you got to get your rest, and you got to have some form of exercise."*
> —Mike Ditka

Winning the game of life involves making smart choices and committing to them. You must incorporate foods from the U.S. Department of Agriculture food pyramid. Include plenty of fruits and vegetables in your diet, reduce your fat consumption, your sugar intake, and your consumption of cholesterol, sodium, and saturated fat.

Mental toughness requires a strong conditioning of your mind, as well as your body and your emotional self. The foods listed above will contribute to the health of your body.

In early 2012, Mr. Scott Halford presented an Executive Stamina Workshop to GE Aviation Systems' senior and executive leadership team. He taught us techniques to more effectively use our brain and to reduce levels of dangerous hormones and neurotransmitters. Halford also stressed the effect of a healthy diet on the brain. He recommended superfoods such as nuts and berries, apples, whole grains, and cocoa. These foods are consistent with the recommendations of other medical experts such as Dr. Nicholas Perricone, recently featured on *Oprah*. Dr. Perricone also recommends superfoods like sprouts and yogurt.

Take this away from the second "D" in MAD PRIDE: *You need to be dedicated to a healthy diet if you want a strong mind, body, and spirit.* Healthy foods and adequate sleep increases mental alertness, and your brain will be focused on winning. By committing yourself to eating foods that contribute to a balanced lifestyle, you are positioning yourself to win.

Coach's Chalkboard

1. Commit to a healthy diet

2. Follow the USDA's food pyramid recommendations

3. Lower your consumption of fatty foods, sugars, and sodium

4. Reduce your cholesterol

5. Incorporate superfoods, such as berries and nuts, into your diet

Chapter 23:
Energy That Energizes

The experience of a high school football game is indescribable. The *Friday Night Light* series revealed to television watchers across the nation how engaging and intriguing high school football could be. High school football brings the community together.

"They're-un-beat-able, un-de-feat-able. Let's-Go-Hus-kies!" The cheerleaders exclaim.

Cheerleaders are entertaining and exciting to watch. They're not just eye candy. They serve an important purpose. Cheerleaders use their energy to convey school (or professional) team spirit by incorporating dances and cheers to draw in the crowd. They use their energy to energize you, the spectator. Cheerleaders use this energy to propel the football players' energy to the next level.

As onlookers, the spectators and cheerleaders are *with* the players. We can use our energy to fire them up. Have you ever been to a game and just felt an overwhelming amount of energy emanating from the crowd? It's incredible. While people have differing opinions on whether home-field advantage really makes a difference, one thing is true for sure—*Teams do get energized from the energy of the people around them.* Home-field advantage might not affect the outcome of the game, but it drives the players to *want* the win more.

Great athletes do the same thing on the field. From the moment they step onto the turf, their actions speak to the enthusiasm. These players bring their energy into the game and use this fuel to execute the team's playbook. This energy is contagious and amplifies the energy within the rest of the team.

In other words, *great players use their energy to energize.*

This principle helped advance my career in many different jobs because it distinguished me from other leaders and team members. During a performance review, I asked my boss for some feedback on what people said about me. People consistently said two things: *She is not an avionics expert. She knows how to get things done.*

Avionics Systems were not my expertise. I possessed only an elementary knowledge of systems such as flight management computers and flight data recorders. I had joined the company the previous year and was learning a new portfolio. But I didn't need to be a system expert. Football taught me what I needed to succeed. I needed to develop a team of experts that were *with me.* By knowing who my go-to guys were, I made first downs. I positively impacted the business, and my performance evaluation reflected my value. Other senior leaders referred to me as a "breath of fresh air." I reinvigorated activities that currently were stagnant.

My successes would not have been possible if I didn't have a team of wide receivers, lineman, centers, guards, tackles, and tight ends helping me to advance the ball. When identifying who is on your team, keep in mind that these individuals do not need to be your direct reports. None of the players on my squad worked for me. In our organization, cross-functional teams were a way of doing business. It was expected that employees would be put on teams with people from other departments. I pulled in those individuals who I thought would be the most value-added for the project.

In order to succeed in my new position, I needed teammates that were passionate about achieving these business goals. We didn't always agree and engaged in healthy debates along the way, but that is part of playing the game. When determining who is *with you* from who it not, don't be quick to label people who disagree with you as *dead weight.* These individuals may bring a valuable perspective to the situation that can help you determine a better solution forward.

Once I distinguished who *was with me* from who was merely *dead weight,* I needed to use my high level of energy to excite my teammates. As a team, we defined what winning meant. Acting upon a common vision, we developed the playbook. Then we executed it. As a football player inspires his team to want to win, I inspired my team to want to be successful.

This principle holds true outside of the career setting as well.

In 2012 the FHN football team wanted to impact the community in a larger way. The Huskies partnered with Building Homes for Heroes (BHH), a national nonprofit that builds or modifies homes to meet the needs of critically wounded veterans.

Winning: Fundraise over $10,000 for the 2012 football season
Playbook: TBD

This was the first year FHN was involved in this project. We wanted it to be a partnership for years to come. All members of the FHN BHH Steering Committee were fired up. We knew what the goal was. We needed to develop the plan. Everyone eagerly shouted out thoughts on how to move the ball forward. We captured the game plan. I was excited. My teammates were passionate to see this effort succeed. We spread the word about this fundraiser.

Members of the community quickly got involved. It was working—*our energy was energizing others.* Husky families were fired up.

This fundraiser encompassed more than raising money. We wanted to honor veterans for their unselfish sacrifices in defending our nation—our land of the free. The Huskies would do this by playing their final game in camouflaged jerseys, provided by former Husky and current Oakland Raiders' offensive tackle, Jared Veldheer.

The event on October 19, 2012 was unforgettable. Veterans from the Grand Rapids Home for Veterans joined us for the game. The halftime show included a special band performance and a check presentation to BHH for over $13,000. The night was even more memorable because the FHN Huskies won that game 39–0. This event was successful because the leaders had energy that energized others.

Many qualities separate the great athletes from the good, the bad, and the mediocre. MAD PRIDE sums up these elements. These personal traits are a *must* if you want to move down your life's field and get into the end zone. It requires training hard—mentally, physically, and emotionally. But the harder you train, the harder you'll be to beat. You'll be able to effectively move the ball—scrambling around the blitz, navigating through the blindside, and creating your own holes. When it's game time, you'll be fired up, and you'll be ready to win. Train like an athlete and have MAD PRIDE!

Coach's Chalkboard

- Great athletes have energy.

- They know how to use that energy to energize their team.

- This energy drives the playbook, moves the ball down the field, and wins games.

"If you train hard, you'll not only be hard, you'll be hard to beat."
—Herschel Walker

At one point in their career, most professional football players have fallen under the umbrella of free agency. The NFL structure consists of five classes of free agents with many subclasses. While this construct might seem complicated, the definition of a free agent can be described in simple terms. *A free agent is a player not currently under contract.*

Every player wants to secure a spot on a football roster. Free agents train hard to achieve this goal. They focus on building their brand. It's what distinguishes them from others and increases their chances to succeed. Free agents work tirelessly to define and promote themselves. You can learn an important lesson from these athletes. *Train hard to ensure you are marketable. Showcase your value.*

Brand You author Tom Peters is an expert in branding. Regardless of your age, your position, or the industry you work in, Peters explains how everyone needs to understand the importance of branding. To be in business today, your most important job is to be the lead marketer for the brand called You. Free agents and great athletes grasp this concept and use it to their advantage. Now it's your turn. Play your game like a free agent and build

> *"It all matters…everything you do or choose not to do communicates brand value and character."*
> —Tom Peters

your brand to be one worthy of mentioning. If people understand the value you bring, opportunities will come your way.

"Check Your Ego" emphasized self-awareness. This is an important step in developing your personal brand. You need to take a hard look at yourself and identify what you want your brand to be. Ask yourself the following questions:

- What sets me apart from my peers and colleagues?
- What characteristics or qualities do I possess that make me unique?
- What do I want my name to be synonymous with?
- What am I known for?
- How well am I known?
- What am I most proud of?
- What's my personal definition of success? What does winning mean to me?

Look within yourself and identify what makes you stand out from the rest. Take Chicago Bear Devin Hester for example. Widely considered the strongest and best special-teams player in the history of the NFL, he currently holds the league record of seventeen return touchdowns. Since joining the Bears roster in 2006, he has proven to be an invaluable asset on special teams and remains atop the Bears' depth chart. His speed, agility, and flexibility make him an unstoppable force on the outside lane. This defines his brand.

Now it's your turn. What defines yours?

In Harvey Coleman's book *Empowering Yourself, The Organizational Game Revealed*, he introduces the P.I.E. model. He asserts that career success is based on three key elements:

1. **Performance:** this encompasses the day-to-day work you're tasked with and the quality of the results you deliver.
2. **Image:** this involves what people think of you. Others perception of you influences your personal brand. Do you maintain a positive attitude? Do you create solutions, or do you institute roadblocks?
3. **Exposure:** In order to get ahead, others need to know about you and what you do. Is your senior management aware of your accomplishments? Are you recognized as an expert by others in your industry?

His model suggests that ten percent of career success is based on performance, thirty percent is based on image, and the majority comes from the individual's amount of exposure. These three elements form your reputation and your brand, which are critical to advancing your career downfield.

"Move the Ball" focused on the importance of execution. Performance is your ticket into the stadium. You must execute if you want to achieve your goals. If people know you are the go-to-guy (or gal) and can deliver results, this forms the basis for your career growth.

I am a member of the GE Women's Network Steering Committee for the Grand Rapids plant. In 2012, GE Corporate gave us a target for our group to raise $5,000 for the Society of Women Engineers Scholarship fund. We held small fundraisers throughout the year, which got us to the halfway point. Time was running out. We needed a larger-scale fundraiser if we wanted to meet our goal. I volunteered to lead our final campaign, a silent auction and a networking happy hour with company executives. A small team worked countless hours alongside me to ensure that all details were addressed. The big evening turned out to be a night to remember, and we raised over $3,000.

We had done it. We met our target! We won. Shortly thereafter, I was awarded the GE Women's Network Hall of Fame Real Hero award. My ability to execute activities like this fundraiser played a role in my selection. People take notice when you and your teams perform.

Your image also plays a factor in defining your brand. Appearances and perceptions *really* do matter. When people describe quarterback Peyton Manning, the responses are generally positive. He has been a respected NFL player for many years and not only for his stats. He proactively reviews game film and studies how he can improve. He trains hard and is known for his professionalism and his leadership. When others think of you, what thoughts come to mind?

Perceptions can open doors for you and can also close them swiftly. How you communicate with people and how you carry yourself makes a difference. Be sure your actions are consistent with the image you want to portray. Keep your ego in check, and don't play dirty.

The amount of exposure you receive is the largest wedge of the P.I.E. model. While your brand is partly defined by your ability to perform and your reputation, the extent of your visibility is critical to crossing the professional goal line. If you want to advance your career, exposure is important both inside your company and out. You must identify projects to get you in front of your organization's management. That's a no-brainer. Look for those opportunities.

It's also required that you stay visible within your industry. Your next career move might be on a different team. You must remain noticeable and engaged in events like tradeshows and conferences. Free agents are out there, building their network and proactively working toward their next opportunity. Performance will only get you so far. You must focus on building your brand.

Free agents are motivated to perform because their future is unknown. These athletes are part of a squad today, but tomorrow could be another story. You must treat your life as if the same was true. Focus on developing your brand, and stay marketable. Play your career game like a free agent, and you'll move the ball.

Coach's Chalkboard

- Stay current, stay marketable.
- Performance is only a small sliver of the career advancement pie.
- Focus on your reputation and build your brand.
- Build exposure opportunities into your playbook.

Chapter 25:
Don't Just Be A Player

"I've always tried to coach people the way I would like to be coached; positively and encouragingly rather than with criticism and fear..."
—Tony Dungy

The objective of any game is to win. In your life, the goal is no different. You want to triumph and be successful. But while your personal accomplishments are important, you must look beyond that. Success should not solely be defined by what you have achieved. Rather, it should also be measured by the impact you make in other people's lives.

Football is a game of teamwork. So is life. Just as others have been *with you*, you must be *with others*. Reflect back for a moment. Do you remember the elementary school teacher who wanted you to succeed and went out of his way to help you? What about that boss who developed and promoted you? Throughout your life, there have been people who have worked to help you move the ball. They have been unselfish and caring. Now it's your turn.

Rule #1: Don't just be a player, be a coach and a teammate.

Part of what makes great athletes and leaders stand out is their willingness to get involved. They want to make a positive impact on others. You need to do the same. Identify individuals or a group whose direction you can influence. Help them get to their next first down. I'm not asking you to change the world. Rather, I'm suggesting you look outside your desires and help others realize their dreams. As the old adage goes, "You may only be one person to the world, but you may also be the world to one person."

Ask yourself, *What have I done today to make a difference for someone else?* If the answer is nothing, then reevaluate your game plan. Make the commitment to help others succeed. You'll find the experiences fulfilling and satisfying.

I was fortunate that I started building my network early in my career. This was before the days of social media resources like LinkedIn and Facebook. Back then, getting connected was much more time consuming. While interacting with others came naturally for me, it took years for me to realize an important lesson: *There were people in my network who were willing and able to help me advance the ball.*

As a career professional in my mid-twenties, I looked for opportunities to meet with executives often. If I knew someone was visiting Southern California, I made an appointment to connect. Each person I met with was diverse in his or her experiences and accomplishments, but yet they all asked me one similar question.

"What can I do for you?"

Why are they asking me this? I wondered. Were they questioning my intentions for meeting? I didn't understand. I did *not* want to give the appearance that I wanted something from them. I didn't schedule these discussions to ask for help or to use them for favors. I genuinely wanted to talk and learn from their experiences—that was all. Because I never understood why these executives asked me this question, I was never prepared with an answer.

However, one day, the puzzle piece fell into place. I finally

> Great athletes don't just play the game; they act as coaches and teammates as well.

got why I was repeatedly asked this question. These executives weren't simply players in their game. They *wanted* to help and filled a spot on my roster, too. They were there to play alongside me as well as to act as my coach when I needed one.

As I progressed in my career, I often recalled these instances. These executives showed me what playing life's game is really about: *helping others succeed.* Today, I mirror their actions, and so should you. While our goals are important, they're not the only ones that matter. In the professional setting, I make it a point to ask others what I can do for them. I *want* to help others, just as others helped me. This principle is not only relevant to the work environment. It applies to your personal life too. Make it part of your daily plan to help someone else. Don't just be a player.

Rule #2: Get involved in your community or support a cause. Be a champion who drives to make a difference in the lives of others.

The National Football League encompasses more than the game of football. While this organization governs the professional sport, it also has created programs to benefit communities across the nation. For example, it started the *NFL Play 60* campaign which was designed to tackle childhood obesity and promote an active lifestyle for kids. During a time when one-third of children in American are either obese or at risk for obesity, the NFL realized that something must be done.

Currently, only eight percent of elementary schools provide daily physical education to students. Initiatives like *NFL Play 60* encourage everyone to get involved and promote active lifestyles for kids. While formal events are held with NFL players and staff, this is only one aspect of the program. Parents, educators, and ordinary people can partake in less-formal activities to further this movement. It can be as simple as reminding kids to exercise for sixty minutes a day, or more structured through an actual fitness package. A plethora of tools are provided for individuals to get involved. Anyone can make these children's lives healthier. And it's fun.

Rule #3: Helping others is good for your mental, physical, and emotional being.

In life, there are times to be serious, and there are times to relax. We must work hard, play hard, and always make time to laugh. Helping others is a plus because it fuels your ambition and drives your determination. It gives you renewed energy and motivates you to move your ball forward. "Check Your Ego" focused on the essentials of a proper attitude. Being positive is a key component of your outlook. When you support others, it not only affects your recipients in a positive manner, but you as well. You become stronger and have optimism to continue toward achieving your life goals.

Every year I volunteer with a nonprofit organization called Volunteer Income Tax Assistance (VITA) which provides income tax assistance to low-income individuals. I prepare tax returns for people who are committed to their jobs and dedicated to their loved ones. While our financial assets may be dissimilar, we are alike in many ways. Each of us has families to support and bills to pay. We are all responsible people and promptly file our income tax returns. Every dollar the tax code provides back to us is significant.

A couple of years ago, a charming older woman walked over to my tax station. After talking for a couple minutes, I learned she worked fulltime to support her young grandson and her lazy, unappreciative, thirty-something daughter. I was outraged to learn that her daughter, who was in good health and capable of working, had grossed a mere few hundred dollars that year. This placed an undue burden on this grandmother to support her family.

The woman was ready to file her tax return as *single,* which would yield her roughly a one thousand-dollar refund. Under her circumstances, I knew she met the criteria to file as *head of household.* By filing her return under this status, she received a refund exceeding five thousand dollars. Though this is not a petty amount for anyone, for a sixty-something-year-old woman earning less than $40,000, this extra money was substantial.

I found it rewarding that I could help her and other strangers receive the maximum refund allowed under the tax laws. Every time I filed a return, a warm and positive energy surrounded me. Getting money back for others not only lifted their spirits, but lifted mine too. I was energized to do more for others and myself. It drove me forward toward my next first-down marker. When you know you have helped someone, how does it make you feel? Is it the same feeling?

Rule #4: Do something good for others unexpectedly.

Both the *NFL Play 60* campaign and my VITA volunteer work are planned-out programs. Being a teammate and a coach is not always a structured activity. You can give to others unexpectedly. It doesn't take much to be on someone else's squad. Simple gestures like exhibiting a positive attitude or providing words of encouragement can make a difference to someone. Grandiose plans are unnecessary. Do not underestimate the impact of little actions. They can go a long way.

> *"There is no exercise better for the heart than reaching down and lifting people up."*
> —John Holmes, Author

One of my coworkers recently lost his sixteen-year-old son in a car accident. Though I was not close to this individual or his family, I wanted to let him know that I cared and was there to support him. I sent him an e-mail expressing my condolences. Then I went on with my daily activities.

Months later, my colleague stopped me in the hallway and said that he was glad to see me. I didn't know why.

"I want to thank you," he said. After his son had passed away, when he was in a time of indescribable pain, my e-mail had made a difference to him. This unplanned gesture only took seconds for me to write, but it had affected him in a significant way. This was inspiring. I was glowing inside, and our exchange gave me extra energy to get through the rest of what had been a chaotic workday.

Rule #5: Be the coach and help people see through their options and develop their playbook.

Each of us needs others to help us see our way into the end zone. A coach does just that. He gives us perspective and helps us develop our playbook. Now it's your turn to be the coach. Every now and then, you'll come across people who lack direction or are insecure. Sometimes, they're afraid of the unknown—of playing in the gray zone. As a coach, you can give them different viewpoints and help them explore options. You can show them how the impossible really can be possible. Your insights will help others improve their plans and progress toward their goals.

In elementary school, parents volunteer to coach their kid's sports teams. While some are driven by a desire to win the game, great coaches know the objective is more than a victory. The role of the coach provides the opportunity to influence and shape others. Coaches provide encouragement and communicate in a positive style. They refrain from criticizing or leading through intimidation. Be a coach for others in both the career and personal settings. Adopt the same approach as great coaches.

Adopt this same approach in your life. As a coach, you need to inspire others and provide reassurance. Help others bring out their best and realize their greatness. With your support, others will achieve the outcomes they desire the most. It's the right thing to do and also gives you a refreshing feeling knowing you've helped another person reach their dreams. Be sure to do it, and do it often.

Life is similar to football in many ways. Defenders in both games come at you from all angles. While you want to achieve your goals, don't forget about the other players trying to play their game who may be struggling to maneuver down their field. There are people who need you to be *with them*. They need your support. Take off your player jersey and be a coach. Make time to wear someone else's uniform and be a member of their team. Remember that winning is not only measured by how many touchdowns you score, but also by how many times you help others cross their goal line.

Coach's Chalkboard

- Don't just be a player; be a coach and a teammate.

- Just as others have been with you, you must be with others.

- Helping others is good for your mind, body, and spirit.

- Get involved in your community or support a cause.

- Give to others unexpectedly.

Chapter 26:

It's Game Time—Get Fired Up!

"The ones who want to achieve and win championships motivate themselves."—Mike Ditka

Great athletes train for every game. From the moment they step onto the field they're mentally, physically, and emotionally ready to win. Now it's your turn to enter the stadium.

This book has prepared you for the victory. It has thrown a lot at you around three main themes: planning, acting, and believing. Winning in life's game starts with *you*. Look in the mirror. Are you *with you*? Are you fired up? Do you possess an energy level that will energize your team? I hope so because now it's game time. Get ready to score.

First, you must be committed to this journey. Are you ready to put in the hard work and sacrifices needed to execute your playbook? This game is a tough one, so be patient and see it through to the end. Beating life's challenges is not stress-free and requires pushing yourself into uncomfortable and unfamiliar territory. It's a necessary part of succeeding. Old practices won't get you where you want to go. Changing some of your behaviors is required. Your ego has to be in check and a positive attitude must dominate during every quarter of your game.

Second, you need to surround yourself with a team of winners. You cannot achieve your goals on your own. You need teammates to keep you grounded, hold you accountable, and help you move downfield. Know who is *with you* and cut *who is not*.

Third, you are in command of your destiny and your happiness. While you cannot always control what opponents may tackle you, you can control how you respond. You must remain positive and have the courage to continue playing. Negativity breeds sadness, stress, resentment, and an unproductive outlook on the game. Refrain from negative thinking. Great athletes don't waste their time on it and neither should you.

As the quarterback in your life, realizing your dreams begins with *you*. Don't look for others to kick you in the butt. You must motivate yourself. Winners inspire themselves and so should you. When you believe that you can achieve, your daydreams become reality.

What does winning mean to you? Look at your list of short-, medium-, and long-term goals. You should have a playbook for each of them. If not, make one. Succeeding in life requires having an edge over others. Your playbook positions you for that edge. By having a plan coupled with an optimistic attitude, your likelihood of forward progress is exponential. Then you must execute your game plan effectively. Concentrate on getting the next first down. Make it happen no matter what. Get out of your personal comfort zone and be comfortable playing the game in the *gray zone.*

Canvas your life's field. Never lose sight of who is out there playing the game. Look at both sides of the line of scrimmage. Don't forget to look for the blitz. It comes fast, and you must be prepared for it. Remember that while you can sometimes read the blitz, you'll never see the blindside. Beware, as both are barriers on your field. Both can also be overcome.

Like it or not, we need challenges like these in our lives to value our accomplishments. We thrive on the feelings of overcoming hurdles. Watch other players' movements. Recognize their blitz, adjust to the blitz, and beat the blitz. When unexpected defenders knock you down, you must rise back up. A great person's true character is displayed when he is able to face adversity and perseveres to achieve his goals. It's your turn to be a great player. Keep charging onward in your game.

Key to your success is a periodic review of your playbook. Make adjustments when needed. Coaches and players know when to alter their plays and so should you. Football and life involve risk-taking. When your field position looks bleak, do not immediately punt. Elite teams don't settle for mediocrity. Neither should you. Test your limits, take chances, and strive to be extraordinary. You must stretch yourself beyond the obvious and have the courage to go for the unknown. Assess your situation and weigh the risks. Then determine your next move.

Whatever the outcome, remember this is *your* game. Own it. Take responsibility for whatever happens. Do not make excuses when the outcome doesn't go according to plan. In football, the game is not over until the game clock expires. In your life, the game is not over until you say the goal is no longer valid. Even if you face a setback, you still control the ball movement and still can win.

Stay in this game. Achieving your goals takes time. Football teams do not become sensational overnight. Neither will you. Patience and perseverance are required if you want to get ahead. You must be flexible in your approach and realize that succeeding requires tolerance and persistence. Remain focused to stomp on any obstacle that stands between you and the goal line. Move the ball and do not lose sight of the next first down marker. Take life one day at a time, and you will do well.

When life becomes overwhelming, recall the football stories shared in this book. Remember how the Xavier Falcons never gave up. With a twenty-one point deficit going into the fourth quarter, the chances of winning seemed bleak. This didn't stifle their resolve. The Falcons stayed committed and, despite the odds, pulled off the victory. When you think accomplishing a goal seems unlikely, let these high school kids inspire you. What seems unachievable *is* achievable if you have the determination to keep playing the game. Don't give up.

In the movie *The Lion King*, Mustafa's ghost tells his son, Simba, "You are more than what you have become. You must take your place in the Circle of Life." The time is now for you to become more than what you have been. You must take your place in the end zone. You are prepared to win. Now you need to train like an athlete and have MAD PRIDE.

Are you mentally tough? Having *mental toughness* requires you to condition your mind, body, and spirit. It gives you an edge and separates you from the others on the field. Others will cave at the sight of challenge, but you are different. For no matter who may try to detract or distract you from accomplishing your goals, you won't let them break you. You'll stay focused and cross the goal line.

Life's challenges can beat you down. Don't let them. Have *ambition with attitude*. Stay motivated and play this game with heart. Even when you are rattled, you must have the willpower to keep going.

Playing this game is demanding. A secret to winning is making the right choices. This starts with having *determined balance*. Make time for your family, for eating right, sleeping, and for some personal time. Build these elements into your playbook. You'll be more effective at moving your ball forward if you do.

Do not overlook the importance of practice. Some good athletes think practice is a waste of time and that is why they never realize greatness. *Practice with purpose* involves committing to your goals and having the discipline to follow through. It requires making lifestyle changes in order to succeed. No successful player or coach achieved his fame without practice, hard work, and sacrifice. They were also unyielding. When life pushed back on them, they had the *relentlessness to rebound.* They never lost sight of the ball and remained focused on getting the next first down. Great players are relentless, and so are you. Use your inner vigor to remain fired up.

Continuous improvement is also a vital component of football and life. Having an *improvement focused* mentality is essential to winning in either sport. Be sure to run the Triple Option when striving for your goals: identify where you need to improve, invent your playbook, and implement it. It's a strategy that can be applied to any situation.

Don't forget that executing your playbook requires energy. A *dedication to a healthy diet* is a given recipe for fueling you up. Include plenty of fruits and vegetables in your diet. Reduce your fat consumption, your sugar intake, and your consumption of cholesterol, sodium, and saturated fat. You also need to eat super-foods to condition your brain. This will help keep your mental toughness strong.

Just as *you* must be driven, *your team* must be motivated. Do you possess *energy that energizes?* Cheerleaders and football players draw people in with their excitement and liveliness. Your enthusiasm must be contagious and must fire up the rest of your team. It takes an energized squad to get you into the end zone. You cannot score alone.

In the career setting, you must play the game as if you were a free agent. Similar to a football player, you need to be aware of your skills, your desire, and your potential. You must actively work to build your personal brand and stay marketable. You need to demonstrate that you can execute. People must recognize you as the go-to player. Know what differentiates you from your competition, and use that to your advantage.

While playing life's game, don't just be a player. You need to be a coach and a teammate. You should not only focus on how you can accomplish your goals. Make an impact on others, and be a community steward. Give unto others, as others have given unto you. Be a champion and help other people win.

Move the Ball has drawn the parallels between life and the game of football. The principles needed to win both games are the same. With these doctrines, you'll drive the ball into the end zone, and you'll be victorious. Winning starts with you having the courage to move forward.

Jerry Lynch retired from Major League Baseball as one of the profession's all-time great pinch hitters. His prowess earned him a spot in the Cincinnati Reds Hall of Fame in 1988. He was known for his skills and his competitiveness. You, too, must be a competitive warrior. Have the courage to be on the field of uncertainty. Play your game with heart and with determination. Do not fear

> *"Confidence is about who puts it on the line, who has the courage to compete like a warrior without the fear of failure."*
> —Jerry Lynch

the possibility of failure. Similar to the way in which you respond to the blitz and the blindside, if you fall down, get back up.

This book has equipped you with the tools needed to succeed in life. You have defined what it means to win and have developed your plans. You know how to execute your playbook. You have the resolution to move the ball. Now it's game time. The ball is about to be kicked to you. No matter where your field position starts, you are ready to maneuver downfield and cross the goal line. You'll achieve your life's goals, and you will score.

If there was one passion I could never give up, it's the game of football. While the quarterback scrambles, missed tackles, and memorable plays make the sport thrilling to watch, football means more to me than a single game. It taught me how to overcome any obstacle and beat life's challenges. It showed me how to be an elite player both on and off the field. Football *is* the reason I get fired up every day. What I learned from football fuels me to achieve more. I have set my expectations high, and I never stop playing until I exceed them.

Ask yourself this. What do you *really* want out of life? Once you have the answer, play your game like a great athlete, have MAD PRIDE, and don't stop driving the ball until you reach the end zone. Your journey will be packed with barriers along the way. You are not alone. It happens to everyone. When you get taken to the ground, pick yourself back up, and rebound. You are a winner, and you will succeed.

I was different than the teenagers in high school. If I could rewind the clock to senior year, I wouldn't change a thing. Even though I was so consumed with football that I chose not to experience going to prom or spending money on a fancy dress and glamorous makeup, I *am* the lucky one.

Football imparted life lessons on me as a young girl. As a teenage mom and a single parent, I could have gone down a different path. No one predicted that I would have accomplished so much. Winning was against my odds. Throughout my life, the blindside struck, and the blitz took me down. I've had my share of relationship and health issues, parenting challenges, resentful co-workers and more. There were often times I could have failed, but football wouldn't let me. It gave me the drive to make possible what others would consider impossible.

Football has now showed you what it taught me. I have followed my dreams and have won. Now it's your turn. I leave you with this.

I am good at what I do, and so are you. I used the game of football to win, and so can you. I believe in you and want you to make your dreams a reality. I am *with you.* Now ask yourself, are *you* with you?

It's game time. So put on your jersey, get onto your field, and move the ball.

About the Author

Jennifer A. Garrett is an author, life coach, and motivational speaker who has a passion for writing and for helping others. She enjoys showing others how they can achieve their dreams and reach greatness. She uses her energy to inspire others through her written work, public-speaking engagements, and coaching sessions.

Jennifer stands out from the crowd because she possesses a rare level of drive and determination. She plays the game of life as if she were on the football field, always focused on getting into the end zone and winning. She settles for nothing less. Throughout her life, Jennifer has proved that she can beat life's challenges and achieve her dreams. As the quarterback in her game, she knows what getting blindsided feels like. She has been knocked down by the blitz. No matter what obstacles have come across her path, she has out-maneuvered them and crossed the goal line.

Jennifer's story is inspiring to those who meet her. Her persistent drive has allowed her to overcome teenage pregnancy and single parenthood. She plays the game of life hard and has completed five college degrees: BS in Electrical Engineering, BS in Biomedical Engineering, Masters of Business Administration, an MA in Communication and Leadership Studies, and a Juris Doctor. She completed her graduate degrees while working full-time and raising four children.

In the business world, Jennifer is recognized as an outstanding leader. She has worked in many challenging positions, where she demonstrated that she could lead teams, inspire others, and deliver results in stressful and challenging environments. She sets high expectations for herself first, never making excuses, and always holding herself accountable.

Jennifer currently works as a marketing director for General Electric. She is responsible for strategy development and military strategic marketing for GE's Aviation Systems' Avionics product lines. Additionally, she is a Judge Advocate officer in the Michigan Army National Guard Judge Advocate General (JAG) Corps, where she advises soldiers on a variety of legal issues and provides them with services such as drafting wills, powers of attorney, and legal representation. In December 2012, Jennifer received the GE Women's Network Hall of Fame "Real Life Hero" Award.

To contact Jennifer, or to sign up for the *Between the Cleats* quarterly newsletter, go to www.jenniferagarrett.com. You can also like her Facebook author page at www.facebook.com/into-theendzone. Follow her on Twitter: @getintheendzone.